IMAGES
of Aviation

THE DOUGLAS
SKYMASTER FAMILY

Meet the family at Douglas Aircraft Company's Santa Monica site in 1953. In the foreground, a DC-7 (N301AA), centre a French registered DC-6, F-BGOD, for Transports Aeriens Intercontinentaux (T.A.I.), and third a DC-4 Cargoliner in United Airlines colours. Beyond that is the updated DC-3S (Super DC-3) in Douglas Aircraft's colour scheme.

IMAGES
of Aviation

THE DOUGLAS SKYMASTER FAMILY

Compiled by
Ken Wixey

TEMPUS

First published 1999
Copyright © Ken Wixey, 1999

Tempus Publishing Limited
The Mill, Brimscombe Port,
Stroud, Gloucestershire, GL5 2QG

ISBN 0 7524 1618 9

Typesetting and origination by
Tempus Publishing Limited
Printed in Great Britain by
Midway Clark Printing, Wiltshire

A TWA DC-4 at Payne Field, Cairo (now Cairo International Airport). It was a DC-4 that inaugurated commercial air services between the USA and Egypt on 1 April 1946.

Contents

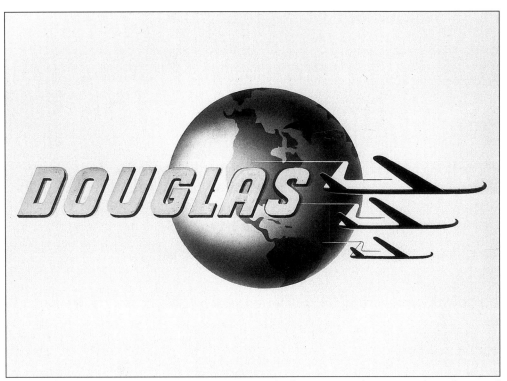

The emblem of the Douglas Aircraft Company which was carried on a number of its civil airliners including the DC-6, DC-7 and DC-3S (Super DC-3).

The Story of the Skymaster Family

Ancestry

In April 1920 a young American aircraft designer, Donald Douglas, arrived in Los Angeles, California, determined to establish his own aviation business. Douglas, a former Glenn L. Martin Co. employee, soon received a contract to produce an aeroplane for David R. Davis, a man desirous of flying non-stop coast to coast across the United States. This resulted in the Davis-Douglas Cloudster, the Douglas company's first aeroplane.

A large single-bay biplane powered by a 400hp Liberty engine, the Cloudster had a top speed of 120mph and a normal range of 550 miles, but 2,700 miles non-stop was attainable with extra fuel tanks installed. A side-by-side two-seater, the Cloudster was also the first aeroplane to successfully carry the equivalent of its own weight.

Designed at the rear of a barber's shop and built in an old wood mill, the Cloudster was completed in just over six months and, on 27 June 1921, the trans-continental attempt started from the USAAC base at March Field. After flying 785 miles at 85mph (in 8 hours 45 minutes), the Cloudster force-landed at El Paso, Texas, when an engine timing gear broke. The aircraft was prepared for a second attempt, but this was cancelled when an Army crew crossed the USA non-stop in a Fokker monoplane.

The Cloudster experience behind him, Donald Douglas competed with top American aeroplane manufacturers in designing a new torpedo-bomber for the US Navy. Douglas won a contract with his DT-1 design, three being ordered by the Navy with two as DT-2s. A further thirty-eight DT-2s were ordered and the expansion of Douglas Aircraft Co. began. In 1924 the US Army, planning a 'round-the-world' flight, ordered a modified DT-2 from Douglas. This proved successful and four more were contracted, all five having provision for twin-float or wheeled landing gear. They had dual controls, Radio Direction Finding equipment (RDF), greater fuel capacity and deletion of unnecessary military equipment. Four aircraft were selected for the flight as DWCs (Douglas World Cruisers). They left Seattle on 6 April 1924, three landing back there on 28 September, one having been forced down *en route*. In 175 days the DWCs had covered 28,900 miles, an epic flight which won much acclaim for Douglas and orders for military variants of the DWCs for USAAC service. The C1 transport variant, one of the first purpose-built cargo aircraft, was issued with Approved Certificate No.14 in October 1927 for commercial use.

The USAAC used Douglas observation biplanes based on the 0-2 version of the Cloudster, the 0-6, 0-7 and 0-8 with different engines and the 0-22, 0-34 and 0-38 with modified airframes. Export 0-2s went to Mexico, 0-38s to Peru, and Norway

The Douglas Cloudster, the first aeroplane designed and built by Donald W. Douglas. With a 400hp Liberty engine it was to be used in an attempt by David R. Davis to fly non-stop coast to coast across the USA. Test pilot Eric Springer and Davis took off on 27 June 1921, but were forced down near El Paso, Texas, with engine trouble after covering 785 miles in 8hrs 45min at an average speed of 85mph.

received a number of torpedo-bombers. Another customer for Douglas was the US Post Office, which exchanged its ageing de Havilland mailplanes (converted First World War bombers) for the M-series of Douglas mailplanes. Western Air Express possessed a US Mail contract and operated seven Douglas mailplanes on their route between Los Angeles and Salt Lake City. These mail flights were usually at night, often in atrocious weather, and mail pilots performed a very valuable service as well as opening up new routes across the USA.

During the 1920s and 1930s Douglas expanded rapidly and went on to produce the P2D-1 twin-engined torpedo-bomber, a large biplane with twin fins and rudders, and one of their first monoplanes, the Dolphin amphibian. This had a duralumin hull and was powered by two Wright or Pratt & Whitney radials mounted on struts above the shoulder-high wing. The land wheels retracted alongside the hull when not in use. The company built four XP3D-1 twin-engined flying-boats for the Navy, while for Army use Douglas high-wing observation monoplanes emerged. The XO-31 of 1930 was followed by the updated YO-31, YO-31A, YO-31B and YO-31C, which led to the Y10-43 and an order for twenty-four O-43As for USAAC service. The Curtiss Conqueror engine of the O-43A was replaced in the XO-46 with a 725hp Pratt & Whitney radial, ninety O-46As being ordered for USAAC and National Guard service.

Further designs by Douglas in the early 1930s included the twin-engined XO-35 and XO-36, the latter being tested as the XB-7 bomber. The XO-35 became a

Early days in Douglas Aircraft Co's cramped drawing office. Originating at the back of a Los Angeles barber's shop, it moved to a Goodyear Blimp hangar, before leasing redundant film company buildings at Wilshire Boulevard, Santa Monica.

Douglas employees beside a DT-1 torpedo-bomber, a Cloudster derivative. Fifth from left is test pilot Eric Springer. The US Navy officer on his right was visiting Wilshire Boulevard in late 1921/early 1922 to discuss Navy purchase of DT-2s.

Powered by a 420hp Liberty, Douglas DWC/O-5 No.2 *Chicago*, one of the US Army Douglas World Cruisers (DWCs) which made the famous 'Round The World Flight' of 1924. Of four DWCs which left Seattle one crashed and a second was lost at sea, its crew thankfully being rescued. This left the two DWCs *Chicago* and *New Orleans* to complete the epic flight, landing back at Seattle on 28 September 1924. In just over 371 hours actual flying time they covered 28,945 miles in 175 days. *Chicago* was later presented to the Smithsonian Institution, Washington DC. *New Orleans* went to Los Angeles County Museum but in 1957 moved to the USAF Museum at Wright-Patterson Air Force Base, Ohio.

mailplane while seven B-7s flew emergency US Mail services in 1934. An XT3D torpedo-bomber of 1931 was turned down by the Navy, while the Army showed little interest in the XFD-1 two-seat biplane fighter of 1933. In 1934 a Douglas XO2D-1 scout-observation amphibious biplane was built with a large central float and retractable main wheels.

Despite commitments to military aircraft, in 1932 Douglas had accepted the challenge of Jack Frye, Transcontinental and Western Air (TWA – later Trans World Airlines), who wanted American aircraft manufacturers to produce a new fast and safe passenger-carrying transport. By September that year a Douglas design had been accepted and in June 1933 the DC-1 (Douglas Commercial One) was ready. A low-wing twin-engine monoplane, it first flew on 1 July and surpassed any civil aircraft then flying in regard to speed, power, comfort and dependability. Initially two 700hp Pratt & Whitney Hornet radials were installed in the prototype DC-1 (X223Y), replaced later by 710hp Wright SGR-1820-F3 Cyclone radials. An automatic pilot was fitted, while noise and vibration dampers resulted in exceptional quiet and smoothness in flight for up to twelve passengers for whom accomodation was provided. The DC-1 was delivered to TWA in September 1933 and underwent an exhaustive test programme during which a number of distance and speed records were established. TWA ordered twenty production machines as DC-2s with uprated 720hp Cyclones, a lengthened fuselage (allowing accomodation for fourteen passengers and extra luggage space), wheel brakes and a modified rudder. The DC-2 had a cruising speed of 200mph and a range of 1,058 miles. TWA received thirty-two DC-2s, the first of which (NC13711 *City of Chicago*) was delivered in May 1934. Other US airlines soon ordered DC-2s, including American Airways (later American Airlines) with eighteen, Eastern with ten, General with four, Pan American Airways with ten and Panagra with three. Some DC-2s were used by the US Navy as R2D-1s and by the USAAC as C-32s, C-33s and C-34s. Others sold well abroad, KLM of Holland ordering nineteen, one of which, PH-AJU *Uiver*, came second in the 1934 MacRobertson race from England to Australia. It was carrying passengers and 30,000 air mail letters and was beaten only by a special British racing machine, the de Havilland 88 Comet. Other countries purchasing DC-2s included Australia, Austria, China, Czechoslovakia, France, Germany, Japan, Poland, Spain, Switzerland and Russia.

When American Airlines president C.R. Smith requested a luxury DC-2 in which sleeping accomodation was provided, the Douglas team produced the DST (Douglas Sleeper Transport), a revised DC-2 with a longer, wider and deeper fuselage in which accomodation provided for seven upper and seven lower berths plus a private cabin up front. Wingspan was extended, a revised fin and rudder fitted and power again uprated by either two 1,000hp Wright Cyclones, or Pratt & Whitney Twin Wasps.

Douglas Aircraft further modified the DST by removing the sleeping berths, which provided an alternative three rows of seven seats apiece in the fuselage. The DST was redesignated DC-3 and was to become immortal as perhaps the most famous transport aircraft of all time, whether as the Dakota or C-47 Skytrain (or 'Gooney Bird'). The prototype DST (X14988) first flew on 17 December 1935, but only thirty-eight were completed as the demand for DC-3s from numerous airlines was overwhelming. It was realized that a DC-3 with a daytime load of passengers contained nearly fifty per cent more capacity than a DC-2. It was larger, faster, more luxurious and standardized components lowered the maintenance costs and improved safety records. Travelling time from coast to coast in the United States was cut to fifteen hours at a cruising speed of between 165 and 180mph. Even when powered by uprated 1,200hp Cyclones or Twin Wasps, the DC-3 was still operable at two-thirds the cost of a DC-2. It was American Airlines' C.R. Smith who stated: 'The DC-3 freed the airlines from complete dependance upon government mail pay. It was the first aeroplane to make money by just hauling passengers'.

When DC-3/C-47 production ceased, 803 had been produced as purely commercial types and 10,123 as military transports, with production at Douglas plants in Santa Monica, Long Beach and Oklahoma City. In the 1950s Douglas attempted to modernize the DC-3 with their refined Super DC-3, which possessed a longer fuselage, increased wing sweepback, taller squared-off fin and rudder, extended dorsal fin and more powerful 1,475hp Wright engines. But airlines were now after new designs with greater seating capacity, tricycle landing gear and four engines. A few Super DC-3s went to Capital Airlines, but most were delivered to the Navy as R4D-8s or the USAF as C-129s.

In the meantime Douglas continued their military contracts, the B-18 bomber, based on the DC-3 and named Bolo, being the subject of a production order for 133 machines.

A further 177 B-18As followed with power-operated nose turrets (in Royal Canadian Air Force service they were named Digby), while another development emerged as the B-23 Dragon. The giant XB-19 four-engined bomber first flew on 21 June 1941 and was then the largest American bomber to have flown. It had a wingspan of 212ft, length 132ft 2in and a height of 42ft 9in, but did not reach production status.

A Douglas passenger flying-boat known as the DF flew in 1936 as a potential type for Pan American Airways. It was hoped the airline would show interest in the aircraft to complement its long-range Martin M-130 four-engined clipper boats. The DF had two 1,000hp Wright Cyclones, but PAA did not require a twin-engined type, and consequently the two DF-151s and two DF-195s built ended up as pairs in Japan and Russia respectively.

In 1937-1938 Douglas took over Northrop's E1 Segundo plant and with it the single-engine A-17 attack bomber, which housed a two-man crew beneath a glazed canopy, was armed with four wing-mounted guns, a flexible gun in the rear cockpit and carried a 1,100lb bomb load on racks beneath the centre-section. The A-17 had a fixed landing gear, but A-17As used a retractable type. As the Douglas 8As, many of these attack bombers were exported to Argentina, Canada, England (RAF Nomad), Iraq, Holland, Peru and Sweden, the latter building them under licence as the 5B and 5C with Bristol Pegasus engines, for the Swedish Air Force.

During 1938 Douglas received an initial order from France for 105 DB-7 twin-engined attack bombers. Powered by 1,200hp Pratt & Whitney twin Wasps, these carried a crew of four, had a top speed of 295mph and carried a 2,000lb bomb load. At the outbreak of the Second World War a further 270 DB-7s were ordered by France, but over 160 had still to be delivered when France fell and these were diverted to Britain for RAF service as Douglas Boston Is. These were used as trainers, Mk IIs which followed becoming Havoc night fighters and intruders, while some 780 Mk IIIs with 1,600hp Wright Cyclones, improved bomb-aiming position and enlarged fin and rudder, were delivered direct to the UK from Douglas and used successfully as RAF day bombers. These were followed by over 250 Mk IVs and Vs with power-operated gun turrets. DB-7s also flew with the RAAF, USAAF (A-20) in Europe and the Pacific, while many went to Russia's Red Air Force.

Two well-known US Navy types by Douglas which participated in the Second World War were the SBD Dauntless dive-bomber and TBD Devastator torpedo-bomber. Dauntless production began in 1939, with initially fifty-seven SBD-1s going to the US Marines and eighty-seven SBD-2s to the Navy. The more heavily armed SBD-3 with self-sealing tanks appeared in 1941, 584 of these being produced before the SBD-4 arrived with a revised electrical system. The US Navy received 780 of this variant before the more powerful SBD-5 was produced, the Wright Cyclone engine having been uprated to 1,200hp. The Douglas plant at Tulsa built 2,049 SBD-5s for the Navy and nine of this version went to Britain's Royal Navy, but they were not used operationally. When the SBD-6 emerged it had a 1,350hp Cyclone engine and Tulsa built 451 of these. The Dauntless also served in the USAAF, 900 being delivered as the A-24 (168 A-24s; 170 A-24As and 615 A-24Bs).

Douglas first produced their TBD Devastator torpedo-bomber in 1935, it being the first carrier-borne monoplane built for US Navy service. The prototype XTBD-1 (BuNo 9720) first flew on 15 April 1935, and after successful naval trials a production order was received for 129 TBD-1s powered by the 900hp Pratt & Whitney R-1830-64 Twin Wasp. In the Pacific War Devastators were active against Japanese naval forces, but after suffering heavy losses at Midway, the type was used as a trainer.

The Douglas DC-5 civil transport made its first flight on 20 February 1939 powered by two 900hp Wright R-1820-G Cyclones. Designed for short-haul routes the DC-5 was of shoulder wing configuration, featured several DC-2/DC-3 components, a DB-7

Military variants of the DWCs included this C1 transport as ordered by the Army in 1925. The first Douglas military transport, it had a 420hp Liberty engine. The C1 was issued with commercial Approved Certificate No.14 in October 1927.

Similar to a DWC this US Army DOS observation biplane (later O-5) was one of six built. With a 420hp Liberty engine and two 0.30in machine-guns in the rear cockpit, it flew with the 2nd Observation Squadron, Kindley Field, Corregidor.

A Douglas O-2B observation biplane, one of six fitted with dual-controls as a command aircraft or two-seat trainer. The engine was a 435hp Liberty. Standard armament and the bomb racks were removed from this variant.

style fin and rudder and tricycle landing gear. Some DC-5s went to US airlines and Holland's KLM, but Douglas military demands greatly restricted DC-5 production. Some flew with the Navy and Marines as R3D-ls and R3D-2s respectively.

The DC-4E Super Mainliner

By the end of 1935, even before the famous Douglas DC-3 transport had made its initial flight, plans were afoot at United Airlines for a four-engined transcontinental passenger transport capable of non-stop flights between cities like New York, Chicago, Los Angeles and San Francisco. These ideas were passed to Douglas Aircraft Co., an aeroplane being required with twice the capacity of a DC-3, a cruising speed of 175mph, a range of 2,000 miles, underwing refuelling at 100 US gallons a minute, a retractable tricycle landing gear, cabin pressurization and climate control, hydraulic power-boosted controls, auxiliary petrol-driven motors for generating electric power while on the ground, 115-volt AC power circuit, flush-riveted metal skinning and a 3,000 psi hydraulic system. United agreed to share half the cost of a new design and Douglas went ahead. Persuaded by United's chief, William A. Patterson, four other US major airlines (TWA, American, PanAm and Eastern) financially backed the project.

Work started on the airliner in 1936, the prototype being designated DC-4E (E for experimental) and power provided by four 1,450hp Pratt & Whitney R-2180-S1A1-G Twin Hornet radial engines driving three-blade metal Hamilton Standard hydromatic propellers. Of all-metal construction the DC-4E was a low-wing cantilever monoplane, the wings bearing a marked similarity in smaller proportion to those of the earlier DC-2 and DC-3. The fuselage, a monocoque structure with flush-riveted

Sweptback upper wings, 'N' interplane struts, a corrugated metal fin and a tailwheel in place of a skid identify this as one of two Douglas O-22s built. An NACA cowling covers the 450hp Pratt & Whitney R-1340-9 Wasp radial. It was delivered in 1929.

Designed for maritime patrol, the Douglas P2D-1 was powered by two 575hp Wright R-1820-E Cyclones with Townend rings. An order for eighteen was made by the US Navy and they operated with Patrol Squadron Three (VP-3) until 1937.

aluminium alloy sheet skinning, contained a flight deck for two pilots and flight engineer, while up to forty-two passengers could be carried (a sleeper version carrying thirty overnight passengers was planned) although this was later raised to fifty-two persons. Luxurious facilities were provided and separate compartments for men and women included, as well as the main passenger cabin. The tail unit was unusual in having triple fins and rudders, the central fin being integral with the rear fuselage; the outer fins were fixed at the extreme ends of the horizontal tailplane which featured a marked dihedral. The landing gear comprised two main wheels which retracted inwards to lie laterally within the wing-root wheel wells; the nosewheel, then innovatory in an aircraft that size, was installed beneath the forward fuselage into which it retracted backwards.

The DC-4E, named the 'Mainliner', was a one-off owing to its concept being too advanced even for the American market. Those airlines involved in the sponsorship now doubted the type was viable enough to show a good profit margin. The tare weight was higher than originally estimated, performance left something to be desired, and as a result the DC-4E was abandoned in favour of it being re-evaluated as a basis for a smaller, simpler and less complex aircraft.

The Skymaster Series

When the revised DC-4E layout emerged it certainly lacked the sophistication of its predecessor. Designated DC-4A the new design had no cabin pressurisation, or auxiliary power plant, and a 24-volt DC electrical system replaced the original AC type. Introduced were slotted flaps, internal gust locks, nosewheel powered steering and the use of twin wheels on each landing gear leg. A revised wing profile possessed equal taper to leading and trailing edges, a high aspect ratio and reduced total area.

Basically the wing was of similar construction to the DC-4E, but the fuselage was shorter and of less diameter.

Accomodation was initially for forty passengers by day, or a sleeper version to convey twenty-eight passengers overnight plus baggage, the intended gross weight being 50,000lb. The empennage was completely redesigned, the original triple fins and rudders giving way to a single fin and rudder, while the horizontal tailplane was now minus any dihedral. Also, whereas the DC-4E's main wheels retracted inwards laterally, the DC-4A's retracted forward and up into the inner engine nacelles. The DC-4A was powered by four 1,200hp Pratt & Whitney R-2000-3 Twin Wasps.

US airline interest in the DC-4A was such that by early 1941 substantial orders had been received. However, war was raging in Europe and contracts for warplanes were pouring into American aircraft manufacturers, Douglas being no exception. Even so, when Japan attacked Pearl Harbour on 7 December 1941, twenty-five civil DC-4As were nearing completion on Santa Monica's production line and nine others were under construction. The US War Department immediately commandeered all thirty-four Douglas DC-4As on the line for USAAF service, the first production machine (41-20137) – there was no prototype as such – first flying on 14 February 1942 under its new USAAF designation C-54. The first twenty-four aircraft were quickly modified for military use, extra fuel tanks being installed in the fuselage, which reduced accomodation to twenty-six but increased the range. All remaining nine DC-4As at Santa Monica, plus eighty-eight ordered, were completed as C-54As and were fitted with strengthened floors, wide freight doors and uprated Pratt & Whitney R-2007-7 Twin Wasps.

The second production C-54 (41-20138) was the first of the type delivered to the USAAF, on 20 March 1942. By the end of that year the original twenty-four DC-4As intended for civil use, together with the first production aircraft, had been delivered to the Army Air Force as C-54s, the name 'Skymaster' being adopted. A total of 252 C-54As was produced between Douglas Aircraft's Santa Monica and Chicago factories, fifty-six of these going to the US Navy as R5D-1s.

The first C-54B flew in March 1944 with altered tankage for its fuel system, one of these (43-17126) flying to Britain for the use of Prime Minister Winston Churchill (later Sir Winston). It became EW999, flew with 24 Squadron and then transferred to the VIP Flight of 246 Squadron. In the USA President Roosevelt also had his personal Skymaster, a C-54A (42-107451) with extra tankage, a stateroom, three conference rooms, a sleeping cabin with bunks and an electric lift for conveying the President's wheel chair to and from the fuselage. Nicknamed 'Sacred Cow' this C-54A was redesignated a VC-54C and made several noteable flights.

The C-54D was similar to the C-54B, but had uprated 1,350hp R-2000-11 Twin Wasps. Several were modified for special roles, like the SC-54D (later HC-54D) Searchmaster for the Military Air Transport Service (MATS) air-rescue service, TC-54D multi-engine crew trainer, AC-54D (later EC-54D) airline evaluation variant, VC-54D staff transport and the WC-54D weather and meteorological reconnaissance version. All 380 C-54Ds produced came from the Chicago plant, eighty-six going to the US Navy as R5D-3s.

Santa Monica built 125 C-54Es with major tankage alterations, increasing fuel capacity to 3,520 US gallons. Interior modifications facilitated a quick conversion from cargo-carrying to passenger transport and vice versa, the C-54E being capable of transporting 32,000lb of cargo, or fifty troops in canvas seats. Alternatively it could operate as a staff transport conveying forty-four personnel in airline style seats. The US Navy received twenty C-54Es as R5D-4s.

The final military Skymaster, the C-54G, was akin to the C-54E but operated chiefly as a troop-carrier and was powered by R-2000-9 Twin Wasps. Of 397 C-54Gs

In Second World War olive drab camouflage, a USAAF Douglas C-54 Skymaster is seen here at Prestwick, Scotland, preparing to convey a number of American staff and military personnel on a USA-bound North Atlantic flight, c.1944. In the upper left distance can be discerned three B-24 Liberators, the centre one of which is in RAF Coastal Command colours.

ordered, only 162 were built, the remaining 235 being cancelled with the Japanese surrender. Last military Skymaster (45-636) was delivered to the USAF on 22 January 1946. A few C-54Gs became VIP transports (VC-54G), others SC-54Gs (HC-54Gs), and thirteen went to the US Navy as R5D-5s, mostly for US Coast Guard duties. Some became R5D-5R (VC-54T) transports and a few R5D-5Z (VC-54) staff transports.

Over 220 C-54s flew with US Navy and Marine Corps units, the first being fifty-six R5D-ls (ex-USAAF), some with modified tankage as R5D-1Cs. The R5D-1F was a Navy staff transport (VC-54E from September 1962) a number of which passed to civil operators in post-war years. The Navy received forty-seven R5D-2s (ex-USAAF C-54Bs) some being converted as R5D-2F staff transports and R5D-2Z (later VC-54P). The largest transfer involved eighty-six R5D-3s (ex-USAAF C-54Ds) these operating in several roles, including R5D-3P (RC-54V) photographic variant and the C-54Q, C-54R, C-54S and C-54T, these designations applying after the reorganization of US military aircraft designations in 1962 to any R5D series still in Navy service. Any earlier R5D-ls or R5D-2s then remaining in service became

C-54Ns and C-54Ps respectively. The C-54Q contained retrospective radar equipment in the nose. Twenty R5D-4s (ex-USAAF C-54Es) flew mainly as personnel transports after updating to R5D-4R (C-54R) standard. The Navy version of the C-54G was the R5D-5, but only thirteen transferred.

Experimental Skymasters included the XC-54F paratrooper with special jump doors; XC-54K special long-range transport powered by four 1,425hp Wright R-1820-HD Cyclones; C-54L incorporating a new fuel system; XC-114 with four 1,620hp Allison V-1710-131 Vee-type engines and an extra 7ft added to fuselage length; XC-116, as the XC-114 but employed for testing thermal de-icing systems; R5D-2-2 (BuNo50851) employed at the Naval Test Centre (NATC), Patuxent River, Maryland, on radar equipment trials and development. This machine could be recognized by four large underwing pods and a 14ft long and very thick retractable antenna which, when lowered, lay flush in a faired cradle forming a dorsal hump.

After the war many Skymasters were sold to civil operators, although quite a number remained in miltary service. Ten C-54Ds which had flown in RAF service were returned to the USA and became R5D-3s in the US Navy. Skymasters played an important role in the 1948 Berlin Air Lift, some being designated C-54M and adapted to carry coal. In the Korean War, thirty C-54Es were modifiied for ambulance duties and as MC-54Ms carried out wounded men from the war zone. The USAF Military Air Transport Service (MATS) used some thirty SC-54Ds (later HC-54Ds) on search and rescue duties, the nose profile of these machines being altered in order to accept the installation of new radar equipment. A number of Skymasters continued in US military service well into the 1960s, those C-54Qs (ex-R5D-3s) which operated with the US Navy on long distance flights until nearly the end of that decade flying from bases far and wide such as England, Iceland, Hong Kong and the Philippines.

Skymasters also served in numerous air forces including, Argentina, Brazil, Belgium, Colombia, Cuba, Denmark, Ethiopia, France, Honduras, Mexico, Peru, Portugal, Saudi Arabia, South Africa, Spain, Thailand, Turkey and Zimbabwe.

At the end of the Second World War the cancelled C-54G order left Douglas with a substantial number of partly built airframes and components on its hands. These were quickly incorporated into a revised civil version, the DC-4-1009, a forty-four-seat passenger aircraft with a fuel capacity of 3,592 US gallons. A pressurized DC-4 was promised for later and a DC-4-1037 freighter version made available. However, with some 300 war surplus C-54s ready to be 'civilianized', the new unpressurized DC-4-1009s were not in great demand and just seventy-nine were built between January 1946 and August 1947. No DC-4-1037 cargo version was ordered and Douglas became responsible for the conversion of many ex-USAAF C-54s to civil DC-4 standard, the majority of DC-4s used by the world's airlines being converted C-54s. In total, 1,084 C-54s were built plus the seventy-nine DC-4-1009s, bringing the grand total of Skymasters built to 1,163.

With so many four-engined Douglas machines readily available, the airlines began ordering DC-4s in quantity for the operation of their immediate post-war services. American Overseas Airlines (later part of PanAm) became the first company to employ DC-4s when, towards the end of October 1945, they inaugurated a trans-Atlantic service between New York and London (Hurn Airport), two stops being made *en route* at Gander (Newfoundland) and Shannon (Ireland), the total journey time amounting to 23hrs 48min.

Pan American World Airways (PanAm), with its international network, soon introduced DC-4s on its trans-Atlantic and trans-Pacific routes, this company having had experience with C-54s during the Second World War, when their African Orient Division flew the type on military contracts in the Middle Eastern, African and Asian theatres of war. United Airlines too flew similar military contracts in the Pacific war zone between 1942 and 1945 with C-54s, and after the war purchased a number of ex-USAAF C-54s, which were modified to civil DC-4 standard and placed in service on United's Chicago to Washington service in March 1946. Just over a year later on 1 May 1947, DC-4s were introduced on the airline's California to Hawaii route. Meanwhile Western Airlines acquired some ex-USAAF C-54s, had them converted to DC-4s, and was the first domestic American airline to operate the type, which entered service on 18 January 1946. In March the same year, Northwest Airlines (later Northwest Orient) introduced DC-4s on its newly extended Milwaukee to New York (via Detroit) service, and on 15 July 1947, began using DC-4s on the trans-Pacific route to Tokyo and Manila via Anchorage; a year later the company inaugurated a DC-4 service from Seattle and Portland to Hawaii. Northwest Orient also assisted with the formation of Japan Air Lines (JAL), which officially came into being on 1 August 1951, Northwest supplying the Japanese company with DC-4s and Martin 2-0-2s. First JAL DC-4 (JA6005) was delivered on 2 November 1951.

Delta Airlines had introduced DC-4s on its Chicago to Miami route in November 1946, the first DC-4 for Delta (NC37473) having arrived on 14 December 1945. Philippine Airlines, which had started a trans-Pacific trooping charter with DC-4s on 31 July 1946, used the same type to inaugurate its regular services to the American West Coast and on 6 May 1947, when Philippine Airlines took over the Far East Transport Co., additional DC-4s were acquired to operate the various routes. Cathay Pacific of Hong Kong received its first DC-4 on 7 September 1949 and during the next five years expanded its routes to take in Calcutta, Saigon and Borneo. Soon after the end of the Korean War, DC-4s (leased from Civil Air Transport) were put into service by Korean Air Lines on its first international route to Iwakuni and Tokyo and in 1953 Korean Air Lines were able to purchase their first self-owned DC-4 (HL108).

The DC-4 also saw considerable service in the Middle East, Israel's El Al forming on 11 November 1948, with one DC-4 and two Curtiss C-46 Commando transports. Royal Air Maroc employed DC-4s on its routes to France and other European countries, as well as on domestic services, the first of its DC-4s (F-BELE) entering service in 1953. In January 1954 Air Algerie received its first DC-4 (F-BELD), while in the following August Tunis Air began a service between Tunis and Paris using DC-4s leased from Air France. Together with Union Aéromaritime de Transport (UTA), Air France also leased a number of DC-4s to Air Afrique in 1961, this new airline having been formed as a joint venture by eleven previously French-owned African states. Saudi Arabian Airlines ordered five ex-military C-54s in 1951 and, after conversion to DC-4 standards, the first two machines (HZ-AAG and HZ-AAI) were delivered in June 1952.

In the meantime South African Airways (SAA) had taken delivery of five DC-4-1009s, the first of which arrived on 25 April 1946. These aircraft were employed on the airline's routes to Southern Rhodesia, Mozambique, Europe and eventually Australia. The last DC-4-1009 built, ZS-BMH (c/n 43157) was in fact built for SAA and, together with the other four machines, flew with the airline until replaced in 1950 by Lockheed Constellations. The five DC-4s were then transferred to the South African Air Force (SAAF) and served with 44 Squadron.

European demand for DC-4s was high, the largest initial order coming from Air France for fifteen aircraft, which were registered *en bloc* F-BBDA/BBDO. They flew on Air France's major routes and inaugurated the company's trans-Atlantic service. Scandinavian Airlines System (SAS) began a Stockholm and Copenhagen to New York service with DC-4s On 16 September 1946, and in December following a new route was established to Buenos Aires. Later, in October 1949, a service to Bangkok was inaugurated, but by the time SAS's Johannesburg route was opened in January 1953, the airline's DC-4s were being replaced by the DC-6. Belgium's Sabena airline ordered nine DC-4s (OO-CBD/CBI and CBP/CBR) and on 16 June 1947 the type started Sabena's service to New York via Shannon and Gander. Another Belgian company, Delta Air Transport, operated one DC-4. Air Portugal (TAP) purchased a number of DC-4s to replace its twin-engined DC-3s on European routes and on the airline's regular runs to Mozambique via Luanda (Angola), although this service terminated at Luanda commencing in 1950.

Iberia of Spain employed DC-4s from the mid-1950s on its medium-haul sectors, while Trans Europa, another Spanish operator, bought four DC-4s (EC-BCJ/BDK/BEB/BER). At the same time Italy's Alitalia was operating DC-4s and some DC-6Bs, these having replaced earlier types like the Fiat G.12, S.M 95 and Avro Lancastrian. Other major airlines which flew DC-4s included Ansett-ANA (Australia); Qantas (Australia); Swissair; Martinair (Netherlands); Bergen Air Transport (Norway); Aer Turas Teo (Ireland) and Olympic Airways (Greece). The type went on to serve in many secondary international airlines both in the passenger-carrying and cargo-carrying role, especially in the Central and South American area. In Great Britain DC-4s (mostly ex-C-54 Skymasters of various marks converted to DC-4 standard) flew with British United Airways, Air Charter Ltd, Skyways and IPEC-Air.

The ATL 98 Carvair

A number of Skymasters were converted in Britain to ATL 98 Carvair configuration by Aviation Traders (Engineering) Ltd at Stansted and Southend airports in Essex. Carvairs replaced the Bristol Freighter car ferries of Channel Air Bridge Ltd, and incorporated an entirely new front fuselage, revised fin and rudder, an 8ft 8in increase in fuselage length and a flight deck 6ft 10in higher than that of a normal DC-4. Direct access for motor vehicles was by means of a special loading platform raised on hydraulic arms, the Carvair's entire nose portion swinging open sideways hydraulically. Eventually Carvairs operated with British United Air Ferries; Aer Lingus; Aviaco (Spain); Interocean (Luxembourg); Ansett-ANA Australia; Eastern Provincial Airways (Newfoundland); Nationwide Air (New Zealand) and Falcon Airways (USA).

The Canadair DC-4M North Star

A Canadian version of the DC-4, powered by four 1,420hp Rolls-Royce Merlin 622 or 624 inline engines, was produced by Canadair at Montreal as the DC-4M North Star. The prototype (CF-TEN-X) first flew on 15 July 1946, the original 'Canadian' DC-4 being a Douglas-built C-54G with four Rolls-Royce Merlin 620 engines. The Royal Canadian Air Force (RCAF) ordered twenty-four North Star Mk Is (C-54GM) plus the prototype (RCAF No.17525) These military variants were unpressurized, but Trans-Canada Airlines (TCA) ordered twenty DC-4M-2s from Canadair, this being a civil pressurized variant with square windows in place of the oval type in the earlier model. However, the DC-4M-2s would not be available before the late autumn of 1947 and TCA loaned six of the RCAF's unpressurized C-54GMs designating them DC-4M-1s. These machines (CF-TEK/L/M and CF-TEO/P/Q) began flying TCA's Montreal to London route on 15 April 1947.

A one-off variant, the C-5, was built as a VIP transport for the RCAF and, as well as being fully pressurized, was powered by four Pratt & Whitney R-2800-CA15 radials. Serialled 17524 (later 10000), this aircraft also operated as a long-range crew trainer and remained in service until July 1967. As for the other RCAF North Stars, they were finally withdrawn in October 1966, having given some nineteen years of faithful service, during which they flew support missions in the Korean War and operated with the UNO on several occasions.

Meanwhile TCA's DC-4M-2s commenced flying the airline's intercontinental and long-haul routes in April 1948, including flights to Europe, the USA (including Florida) and Mexico. Four DC-4-1s (a variant of the DC-4M-2) were purchased by Canadian Pacific Air Lines, the first of which, CF-CPI *Empress of Sydney*, was delivered in May 1949. On 13 July this aircraft inaugurated CPA's service to Australia via the Hawaiin Islands and Fiji, while the first North Star service to Hong Kong commenced on 19 September 1949.

Despite Canadian use of DC-4M North Stars it was a Britain's BOAC airline which became chief operator of the type, twenty-two being ordered in July 1948 as the Argonaut class in British service. The Argonauts were pressurized and contained an appreciable amount of British equipment. They were powered by four 1,760hp Rolls-Royce Merlin 626s and had a gross weight of 82,230lb. Accomodation was for fourty passengers and a VIP version was also made available, this VIP arrangement being retained as an alternative later when BOAC's Argonauts were modified to carry fifty-four tourist-class passengers. The first Argonaut (G-ALHC) was delivered to BOAC on 26 March 1949, the last one (G-ALHY) arriving on 8 November the same year. After withdrawal of the BOAC Argonaut fleet (the last was sold in 1960), most went to small independent operators like Air Links Ltd; British Midland Airways; Derby Airways; East African Airways Corp.; Flying Enterprise (Denmark); Aden Airways and others. One or two were delivered to the Royal Rhodesian Air Force, and one Argonaut, G-ALHJ named Arcturus, was retained by BOAC and used at their Heathrow Training School until 1970.

The DC-6 Series

When Douglas Aircraft decided to update their successful Skymaster layout, they produced the XC-112A military transport and considered this suitable as a prototype for their new DC-6 design introduced in 1946. This revised design was faster and more luxurious than the DC-4, and was powered by four Pratt & Whitney R-2800-CB16 Double Wasps. Its cabin was more spacious, the floor level uniform in width and height or virtually its full length, the interior of very high quality, with deeply cushioned seats that lowered to a semi-reclining position by use of a button on the arm-rest, and large rectangular windows were installed. Pressurized and sound-insulated the cabin incorporated automatic air conditioning to control temperature and humidity. The DC-6 featured pre-loaded cargo containers, underfloor baggage compartments, reversible propellers, thermal de-icing for wings, tail unit and windscreen, a ground air conditioning system, double-slotted high-lift flaps and weather-seeking radar. Accomodation was for up to fifty-two first-class or eighty tourist class passengers. Cargo space amounted to 373cu.ft.

The higher powered engines of the DC-6, combined with the new double-slotted flaps (worked in conjunction with a small slat ahead of the main flap), allowed use of the same runways as a DC-4 despite a weight increase to 93,200lb gross. Overall length was 100ft 7in and the wingspan 117ft 6in. Tailplane span on the DC-6 was increased to 46ft 6in, while the height was raised to 28ft 5in due to vertical tail surface modifications.

The maiden flight of the first production DC-6 took place at Santa Monica on 10 June 1946, and by the end of April 1947 the type was in service with American Airlines on their New York to Chicago route and with United Airlines on its transcontinental services, the eastbound flight across the USA now re-scheduled for ten hours. In fact both American and United Airlines had proved their confidence in the Skymaster by ordering, or taking up options, on fifty of the 'improved' version as early as 1944, a further forty being ordered shortly afterwards. This meant these arrangements were agreed between the two airlines and Douglas well over a year before the military XC-l12A (progenitor of the DC-6) took off on its initial flight!

United, having taken delivery of its first DC-6 on 24 November 1946, used the type on its North American routes, and was soon flying them on the San Francisco and Hawaii service. Pan American-Grace Airways flew DC-6s on their Miami to Buenos Aires route, while National Airlines introduced DC-6s on its services to Boston, New York, Miami, New Orleans and Houston.

Delta Airlines, which operated mainly over the eastern half of the USA, received its first DC-6 (N1903M) on 5 November 1948, three machines having been ordered to replace DC-4s. The DC-6s were introduced on the airline's USA services as well as its increasing network covering Cuba, Haiti, Dominica, Puerto Rico, Jamaica and Venezuela. Western Airlines operated a fleet of twenty-seven DC-6s the company's routes taking in thirteen western American states and services to Canada and Mexico. To ensure non-stop Atlantic flights to major Eurpean cities, Pan American acquired a number of DC-6s, the first of which was delivered to the airline on 27 February 1952.

The DC-6 became a popular choice of numerous airlines overseas, Sabena of Belgium being the first European company to operate the type on its Brussels to New York service. Royal Dutch Airlines (KLM) purchased seven DC-6s for use mainly on its south Atlantic route to South America, while Scandinavian Air Lines System (SAS) acquired seventeen DC-6s for its international routes, four of these going later to British Commonwealth Pacific Airlines (BCPA). The Spanish airline Spantax operated DC-6s from 1965 onwards, the type remaining in service for over a decade. Like its DC-4 predecessor, the DC-6 flew for quite a number of years with airline operators far and wide, some of the better known ones including, Aerolineas Argentinas; Aerolineas Peruanas; Aeronaves de Mexico; Aerovias Panama; Air Liban; Alaska Airlines; Alitalia; Braniff International; British United; Cathay Pacific; Cunard Eagle; TAI (France); Trans Arabia Airways; Trans Caribbean Airways and Union Aéromaritime de Transport (UAT), France.

In the meantime Douglas had decided there was room for improvement to the basic DC-6 regarding weight, which could be increased and spread in a revised fuselage intended primarily for freight operations. Power would be in the form of four uprated Pratt & Whitney R-2800-CB17 Double Wasp radials with water-methanol injection resulting in a rating of 2,500hp each. Consequently a freighter version emerged with a fuselage lengthened to 105ft 7in, an extra section being inserted ahead of the wings, while a reinforced floor with upward-swinging large freight doors front and rear on the port side was fitted, cabin window apertures were blanked off with metal inserts, pressurisation of the aircraft was maintained and an improved electrical system installed. Due to the longer fuselage, the wheel base between nosewheel and main wheels was 5ft 3in longer than on the DC-6. Capacity of the freighter, designated DC-6A and named Liftmaster, was 4,942cu ft, the maximum take-off weight 107,000lb, of which 33,027lb was the payload, and fuel tankage increased to 5,525 US gallons.

Prototype DC-6A Liftmaster (N30006) made its initial flight on 29 September

1949, but it was eighteen months before the type was delivered to the first civil customer, Slick Airways, an all-freight line operating out of San Francisco. It received the protoype, re-serialled N90806, on 7 March 1951, and a second DC-6A the following August with four more following later. At first the DC-6A did not appeal to the airlines, but on 16 May 1953 American Airlines received their first example. Thereafter seventy entered service with a number of civil operators including Sabena, SAS, Swissair, PanAm (leased from Slick Airways) which introduced the first civil all-freight trans-Atlantic service on 5 January 1952 with a DC-6A, United Airlines, Aerolineas el Salvador, Aerolineas Nacionales del Ecuador, Europe Aero-Service (France), Fred Olsens Flyselskap, Linea Aerea del Cobre, Saber Air Pte Ltd, Air Afrique, Southern Air Transport, and Loide Aereo Nacional (Brazil), which incidentally received the last DC-6A Liftmaster built on 10 February 1959.

Douglas also produced a quick-convertible (QC) freight-or-passenger variant as the DC-6C – more often referred to as the DC-6A/B. Quite a number of these 'dual-purpose' transports were sold abroad, flying with such airlines as KLM, Alyemda (Yemen), Balair, Lan-Chile, Lineas Aereas Costarricenses, Reeve Aleutian Airways, Transair/Midwest, Pacific Western Airlines and Trans-Mediterranean Airways. Six DC-6As sold to Britain were in fact classed as DC-6Cs and operated with Hunting Clan (later part of BUA) and Cunard Eagle Airways. These six machines flew well into the 1960s, although one (G-AOPM) crashed at Shannon on 26 March 1961. The remaining five went to buyers in Canada, Switzerland, Saudi Arabia and Bermuda, while one (G-APON) was returned to the USA and became N6814C.

More enthusiasm was shown by the US military to the DC-6A, ten being ordered by the Navy as a first contract and delivery commencing 7 September 1951. Navy designation was R6D-1, some being modified as VIP transports (R6D-1Z), however, in the 1962 military aircraft re-designation system, all R6D-1s in US Navy service became C-118Bs. Altogether sixty-five of 166 military DC-6As built served initially with the US Navy, but later forty were transferred to the USAF for operations with the MATS, leaving twenty-five R6D-1s (C-118Bs) in Navy service. The USAF had already been supplied with 101 military DC-6As as C-118As, this designation applying to the transferred Navy machines in 1962. The last C-118A was delivered on 23 January 1956, but later a number of the USAF C-118As were returned to the Navy and had their original BuAer numbers re-allocated to become C-118Bs.

Military DC-6As differed little externally from the civil version, but the 2,500hp R-2800-52W engines were the Double Wasp military version, while the gross take-off weight was increased to 112,000lb, the freighting capacity to 4,677cu.ft and maximum accomodation provided for seventy-six military personnel, or alternatively sixty stretcher cases when in ambulance form. A crew of four or five was allowed for in accordance with the role being undertaken. In total 240 DC-6As were built of which only seventy-four were for the civil market, the rest going to the military.

If the DC-6A was not terribly successful as a commercial type, its immediate DC-6B successor was considered to be an outstanding success. Indeed the DC-6B was in service some five years before the civil airlines purchased any noticeable number of DC-6As. Described in most glowing terms by many operators and thousands of passengers, who flew in comparative luxury as far as airliners were concerned, the DC-6B was looked upon as one of the most successful and economical piston-engined transport aircraft that ever flew.

A passenger version of the DC-6A, DC-6Bs had no front and rear cargo-loading doors, while the specially reinforced floor was replaced by normal cabin flooring more suitable for the requirements of an aircraft designed to initially carry fifty-four passengers. The four 2,500hp Pratt & Whitney R-2800-CB17 Double Wasp engines were retained, while as on the earlier DC-4s and DC-6s, the main landing gear and

UK-registered G-APNO, one of six DC-6Cs used by Hunting Clan in the 1960s. It was fitted with four 2,500hp Pratt & Whitney R-2800-CB17 Double Wasps with water-methanol injection. The cabin windows were blanked off with metal inserts for freighting and the fuselage was longer than the original DC-6. In December 1968 this machine was sold to Switzerland as HB-IBS.

nosewheel retracted forward and upward into the inner engine nacelles and lower front fuselage respectively. The rear cargo door, as fitted on the DC-6A, was replaced by a passenger door still on the port side. There was no forward door that side, but the crew's entry door was on the front starboard side as on previous models. Early production DC-6Bs accomodated up to fifty-four passengers, but seating arrangements on later machines were modified to accomodate fifty-six first-class, or up to 102 tourist class.

The first DC-6B (N37547) made its initial flight from Santa Monica on 10 February 1951, and less than three weeks later, on 29 April, the first fare-paying DC-6B entered service with American Airlines on their transcontinental route. Top speeds and cruising speeds of the DC-6A and DC-6B were similar, being 360mph and 315mph in both models respectively, but the DC-6B had a faster climb rate, longer range of 3,005 miles (4,720 miles on maximum fuel) although the maximum payload was some 3,600lb less at 24,565lb. DC-6A and DC-6B take-off weight was 107,000lb, but the DC-6A was lighter than the DC-6B empty, the tare weights being 49,767lb

Taken on a wet day at Baginton, Coventry, on 11 April 1979, this picture shows a Douglas DC-6B carrying the registration G-SIXB and beneath the cockpit the name *Amalik*. Owned by Bowden Grange Enterprises Ltd at the time, it was on lease to Air Cargo of Switzerland. Fifty-six first class or up to 102 tourist class passengers could be accommodated.

and 55,357lb respectively.

Main attributes which accounted for the great success of the DC-6B was its low maintenance costs in regard to the structure, electrics, hydraulics and other equipment, the comparative luxury enjoyed by passengers and, of course, the trusty and very reliable Pratt & Whitney Double Wasp radial engines. The type was soon in great demand, Douglas Aircraft's order books being well filled to the tune of 288 aircraft as contracts were signed by airlines both in the USA and other countries.

American Airlines, having initiated the DC-6B into service, bought twenty-five of them for use on their large coast to coast domestic network, with main interchange points at Chicago, St Louis and Dallas. DC-6Bs also flew the company's international routes including, Canada, Mexico and Hawaii.

United Airlines purchased forty-three DC-6Bs for use on its domestic services to eighty-two cities in twenty-four American states, later expanded to 118 cities in thirty-two states. International services were flown to Canada and Hawaii, the DC-6Bs operating alongside United's piston fleet of DC-6s, DC-6As, DC-7s, DC-7As and Convair 340s. By then United were increasingly using DC-8, Boeing 720 and 727 and Sud-Aviation Caravelle jets. Another well known US company, Western Airlines, flew some twenty-seven DC-6Bs on their domestic routes from Los Angeles to Mexico City, the West Coast northwards to Seattle and Anchorage (Alaska), eastwards to Minneapolis (St Paul) and westwards to Hawaii.

Canadian Pacific Airways used eight DC-6Bs among other types on its service from Vancouver to Mexico and Peru, and on 3 June 1955 a DC-6B inaugurated CPA's trans-polar route, Vancouver to Amsterdam via Edmonton and Sondre Stromfjord. SAS employed its DC-6Bs on the trans-Arctic run, between Europe, North America and the Far East. These SAS C-6Bs operated out of Copenhagen *en route* for Los Angeles with refuelling stops along the way, recognized as a great step forward in commercial aviation.

European airlines introduced DC-6Bs on their major routes, Swissair being first with DC-6Bs which started flying their trans-Atlantic run in July 1951. DC-6Bs also replaced DC-4s on Swissair's South American route and on the Tokyo via South East Asian service. Other European company's using DC-6Bs included Delta Air Transport (Belgium), Air Portugal (TAP) with leased machines from UAT of France, British United Airways (leased), Caledonian Airways (leased), Olympic Airways of Greece (leased) and JAT of Yugoslavia, which purchased two DC-6Bs and flew them on its routes to Zurich, Paris, Rome, Brussels, Stockholm and destinations in the Middle East.

Worldwide other DC-6B users included, Kuwait Airways (also acquired some DC-6Bs when it took over Trans Arabia Airways); Syrian Arab Airways (later Syrian Air); El Al of Israel; Cathay Pacific; Philippine Airlines; Lan Chile; Northwest Orient; Pan American World Airways and Sabena (Belgium).

The DC-7 Series

At the end of 1951 a new powerplant became available when Curtiss-Wright successfully raised piston engine power by the introduction of compounding. They produced a big eighteen-cylinder double-row radial in which the exhaust gases were diverted to turn three turbines fitted at the rear of each engine. These in turn channelled the extra energy created (some 20% of the thermal normally lost with exhaust gases) through a system of gears to the crankshaft. Known as the Wright R-3350-18DA1 Turbo-Compound the new engine was rated at 3,250hp American Airlines president, C.R. Smith, aware of TWA's superiority on long-haul routes with their Turbo-Compound engined Lockheed L-1049 Super Constellations, prompted Douglas to improve their DC-6B by installing the new Wright Turbo-Compound engines. Douglas were reluctant at first to go ahead, believing the market was already overplayed in regard to the traditional piston-engined types of airliner. However, the company was finally persuaded when American Airlines offered to pay $40 million for twenty-five updated airliners to complement its DC-6 series fleet. This substantial contract paid for much of the development costs, Douglas producing the newly designated DC-7 on a similar basis to the DC-6A and -6B. In the event Douglas sold 338 DC-7 series aircraft, which made a considerable profit for the company.

Directly developed from the DC-6B, the DC-7 had its fuselage stretched by 40in which resulted in an additional row of seats, and although the DC-6B's 5,525 US gallon fuel tank arrangements were retained, a number of design changes were incorporated. These included the use of titanium in 90% of the engine nacelle and firewall construction to increase fire resistance, a strengthened landing gear in which the main units could be lowered at high speed for use as an air brake, a Douglas type carburettor airscoop to prevent ice inducing moisture entering the air induction system, automatic feathering propellers, air conditioning and pressurization automatically controlled in order to provide maximum comfort in all flight and temperature conditions and a complete Freon optional cooling system which provided filtered, cooled dry air to the cabin both in flight and on the ground.

Douglas works drawings showed the constant contour section stretched by 3ft 4in, resulting in an overall fuselage length of 108ft 11in, while the wheelbase between the nosewheel and main wheels had increased to 36ft 1in. Gross weight of the DC-7 was

122,200lb and maximum payload 16,780lb. There was also now 606cu.ft of cargo space and accordingly the landing gear was strengthened to support the extra weight. Other small detailed alterations were carried out but, apart from the added length, there was little externally visible to show the difference between a DC-6B and the revised DC-7 design.

Altogether 105 of the initial DC-7s were sold, with American Airlines adding a further nine to their original order for twenty-five, while United Airlines purchased fifty-seven aircraft, Delta Air Lines ten and National Airlines four. Making its first flight on 8 May 1953 the prototype DC-7 went to American Airlines and the following 29 November was introduced on their New York to Los Angeles service. Time for the eastbound trip was reduced to 8hrs, that for the westbound flight to 8hrs 45min. However, from a passenger's viewpoint, the DC-7 was a retrogade step in comparison to the DC-6B regarding vibration and interior noise level. This was unavoidable with the initial DC-7 design as the Turbo-Compound engines were installed on a wing structure originally designed to withstand vibrations from 2,000hp engines.

Douglas decided to refine the DC-7 aerodynamically and also to provide a longer range for operators like PanAm, who wanted an aircraft which could undertake their New York to London service non-stop. Thus the updated DC-7B was introduced, this being an interim, albeit logical, revision to carry more fuel. To achieve this the engine nacelles were lengthened aft and saddle-type tanks installed in the nacelle extensions. Now the possible maximum fuel capacity of a DC-7B was 6,460 US gallons and, on 13 June 1955, PanAm began a non-stop North Atlantic service with its DC-7Bs. But even then it was found the extra fuel carried still left a capacity margin which was too narrow for safety. Indeed the eastbound flight from London to New York was often forced to divert for a fuelling stop when conveying a full load and facing the prevalent Atlantic headwinds.

The prototype DC-7B (N70D) first flew on 25 April 1955, and in comparison to the DC-7 maximum take-off weight had increased by some 3,800lb and the payload improved by another 1,516lb. Most DC-7Bs were sold to US operators the majority of which declined taking advantage of the extra tankage available. Delta Air Lines purchased eleven including the prototype, one of the last six built for Delta (N4887C) later being sold and modified as a water-bomber to combat forest fires. For this purpose a streamline under-belly pannier was fitted capable of containing up to 2,400 US gallons.

American Airlines bought twenty-four DC-7Bs, Eastern ordered fifty but received forty-nine (one was lost prior to delivery and not replaced), Continental Airlines purchased five, National four, Panagra (Pan American Grace) six and PanAm seven, referring to them as 'Super 7 Clippers', one example (N777PA) being allotted the name *Clipper Jupiter Rose*. The only overseas order for DC-7Bs came from South African Airways, which required the type for its long-distance routes. Replacing Lockheed Constellations on the Johannesburg to London service on 21 April 1956, the SAA DC-7Bs reduced the flying time on this route to 21hrs, seven less than their predecessors. A number of DC-7Bs went to secondary airlines when their service with major operators had finished, among those acquiring the type being Air Fret (France), Sabena (Belgium), Caledonian Airways (on lease for a short period), Internord and Transair Ltd of Canada.

The DC-7 also proved adaptable for freight work, two wide cargo doors on the port side of the fuselage and reinforced flooring resulting in conversion of the DC-7B into a DC-7B/F, or DC-7B Cargo as it was known at Douglas. In addition to twenty-one DC-7Bs modified by Douglas to DC-7F standard, a number of airline operators converted some of their DC-7Bs for cargo work as a new generation of jet transports

The ultimate Douglas piston-engined transport, a DC-7C of KLM Royal Dutch Airlines 'De Vliegende Hollander' flies above a becalmed sea on one of the airline's international routes. Four 3,400hp (take-off) Wright R-3350-18EA-1 Turbo-Compound engines gave a top speed of 406mph and a cruising speed of 346mph. The range with maximum fuel was 5,635 miles.

was introduced for the passenger-carrying duties. Douglas figures showed the DC-7B Cargo having a gross take-off weight of 126,000lb with maximum payload totalling 35,800lb. Cargo capacity was 5,243cu.ft, and the aircraft could fly 2,900 miles (maximum fuel) at a cruising speed of 350mph, the operating altitude being 25,000ft.

Altogether 112 DC-7Bs were produced, 108 for US customers and the four South African machines. The last DC-7B built went to Continental Airlines in March 1958. Strangely, and despite the later date, DC-7s did not actually succeed the DC-6 series on the Santa Monica production line. DC-6As and -6Bs were in fact built side by side with DC-7s, DC-7Bs and the final variant of the DC-7 series, the DC-7C.

Ultimate in development of the Douglas four-engined piston transports the DC-7C came into being mainly because PanAm had proved the shortcoming of the DC-7B in its attempts to combat the worst of the Atlantic weather. Even as they were taking delivery of their DC-7Bs in the spring of 1955, PanAm had already placed an order for fifteen updated DC-7 series, which Douglas promised would be an improvement on the DC-7B. It was envisaged the revised design would have increased passenger accomodation, a larger fuel capacity and, most important, be capable of all-year round non-stop trans-Atlantic flights in both directions. Because Douglas intended the modified layout to be capable of crossing any of the world's oceans to link continent with continent, they appropriately dubbed it in alpha-numerical sequence the DC-7C 'Seven Seas'.

The DC-7C was first in the whole DC-4 to DC-7 family to feature an increase in wingspan, despite a fuselage stretch of nearly 18ft and a gross weight increase of some 53,000lb during development of the entire series. The revised span measured 127ft 6in and was necessary for the installation of additional wing tanks which contained a further 1,365 US gallons of fuel, while at the same time providing extra lift for the inevitable increase in maximum take-off weight. The extended wingspan was provided by incorporating a new centre-section of equal chord and thickness without dihedral. This added a further ten feet to the span allowing the inner engines to be installed 17ft 4in out from the fuselage centre line. This was a bonus, however, as it reduced noise level in the passenger cabin and lessened vibration. The fin and rudder height was also increased giving the DC-7C a total height of 31ft 8in. Payload capacity was increased by stretching the fuselage a further 3ft 4in, this being accomplished by inserting a 'plug' in the constant contour section again, which increased the overall length to 112ft 3in. This additional space allowed accomodation for sixty-two first-class, or up to 105 tourist class passengers, plus a cargo/baggage area amounting to 651cu.ft.

Meanwhile Curtiss-Wright had improved their Turbo-Compound engine so that the R-3350-18EA-1 fitted to DC-7Cs produced 3,400hp for take-off and, with a gross weight of 107,000lb, gave a top speed of 406mph, cruising speed 346mph, range (with maximum fuel) 5,635 miles, or 4,605 miles with maximum payload. Service ceiling was 21,700ft and the maximum take-off weight of a DC-7C stood at 143,000lb, an increase of 17,000lb over the DC-6B, the payload correspondingly rising to 23,350lb, an extra 1,834lb. The eight wing-mounted fuel tanks provided the DC-7C with a maximum capacity of 7,824 US gallons.

The prototype DC-7C took off on its maiden flight from Santa Monica on 20 December 1955, its initial flight test programme revealing the excellent qualities of this revised DC-7 design. Although running costs left something to be desired the DC-7C was nevertheless superior to its contemporaries (Lockheed's L-1649 Super Constellation was not then ready for service), the payload, range and non-stop long-distance capabilities ensuring adoption of the DC-7C by several major international airlines.

PanAm ordered fifteen DC-7Cs in an initial contract, with ten more to follow later. This meant that at one time PanAm were operating twenty-five DC-7Cs, ten DC-7F freighters and seven DC-7Bs. Northwest Orient ordered fourteen DC-7Cs to replace its L-1049G Constellations, the first DC-7C (N284) arriving on 28 February 1957. American Airlines numbered twenty-five DC-7Cs and ten DC-7Fs among its huge fleet, while other USA operators of the type included Airlift International (Miami), Braniff International Airways, Riddle Airlines and Saturn Airways (Oakland).

DC-7Cs sold well in other countries too. In Great Britain BOAC was experiencing delays in the availability of Bristol's Type 312 Britannia and, as a consequence, ordered ten new DC-7Cs from Douglas for delivery during 1956 and 1957. The first arrived on 23 October 1956, the remaining nine machines being delivered between 17 November and 19 April 1957. British registrations were G-AOIA to ...IJ, these aircraft operating on BOAC's major routes until the mid-1960s. The majority were returned to the USA when Vickers VC-1O and Boeing 707 jets replaced them in BOAC. One machine returned to the US as N16465 (ex-G-AOIJ), was a DC-7F freighter conversion.Two other BOAC DC-7Cs were sold elsewhere, G-AOIE going to Caledonian Airways (later British Caledonian) in April 1964. It was sold three years later to Martinair of Holland as PH-SAK. The second ex-BOAC machine (G-AOII), converted to a DC-7F in 1960, was sold to Denmark in June 1965 as OY-KNE.

Another ten DC-7Cs registered in the UK were all acquired by Caledonian Airways Ltd and Trans Meridian Air Cargo Ltd London. The five Caledonian machines came from Sabena (Belgium), while Trans Meridian received five DC-7F freighter conversions all ex-American registered. Dutch based KLM purchased fifteenDC-7Cs and introduced the type on its trans-Polar Amsterdam to Tokyo route in April 1957. Belgium's Sabena ordered ten DC-7Cs for use on its major international routes, while SAS acquired fourteen DC-7Cs, introducing them on its Copenhagen to Tokyo service on 24 February 1957. Swissair, already a DC-6B operator, bought five DC-7Cs to help build up its long-haul European network.

Alitalia of Italy bought five DC-7Cs for its long-distance routes in the early 1960s, and TAI of France (later merged with UAT to form UTA) flew a number of DC-7Cs for a time on its routes to America, Africa, Australia, the Middle and Far East. Spantax of Spain flew four DC-7Cs and two DC-7Fs, while another Spanish company Teca (Transeuropa Compañia de Aviación) used three DC-7Cs. In Holland, Martinair flew four DC-7Cs bought from KLM in addition to PH-SAK acquired from the UK. All had been withdrawn by the end of April 1969. Aer Tufas Teo of Eire purchased one DC-7C (EI-AWG) which they operated alongside their DC-7B/F freighter. Elsewhere DC-7Cs operated with Persian Air Services, Air Trans Africa (PTV) Ltd of Rhodesia, Panair Do Brasil and Japan Air Lines.

By the early 1960s it was obvious the days of four-engined propeller driven airliners were numbered as the big jetliners made their presence felt. This was especially so with the DC-7C which was not such a reliable machine on the whole as the older DC-6As and -6Bs, and was certainly less economical to operate. Thus while numbers of ageing DC-4 and DC-6 series continued in service, albeit with minor airlines and charter companies, the majority of DC-7Cs were either converted to DC-7C(F) or DC-7CF freighters or simply scrapped. Conversion to freighters usually involved fitting strengthened cargo floors and extra large loading doors, fore and aft, on the port side of the fuselage. Douglas carried out major conversion work on DC-7Cs during 1959 and 1960, so that in addition to some US airlines receiving Douglas-converted freighters, several went to foreign customers who wanted the DC-7C/F including, BOAC, KLM, Alitalia and Japan Air Lines.

The conversion of ten PanAm DC-7Cs as freighters was undertaken by Lockheed Aircraft Services, these machines having cargo-type flooring, extra large doors and specially designed cargo handling apparatus. A number of DC-7Cs were also converted by some airlines themselves as either freighters, or as a quick-convertible passenger/cargo type in a the same way as the old DC-6A/B machines had been.

Three French DC-7Cs were modified and flown by UTA in the mid-1960s as support aircraft for French nuclear tests in the Pacific at that time. They were later modified in 1966 by UTA for participation in France's space programme as observation aircraft for satellite-launching, tracking and re-entry. For this purpose the DC-7Cs, re-designated DC-7AMOR (Avion de Mesure et d'Observation au Receptacle) incorporated a large radome atop the centre of the fuselage as well as direction-finding equipment mounted at the port wingtip. There was also a radome beneath the forward fuselage and Doppler radar installed under the rear fuselage. These DC-7AMORS were fitted out with special electronic and radar equipment, with observation points being provided in five positions, one each side of the fuselage ahead and behind the wings and one on top. A flight crew of two pilots, navigator and two flight engineers was carried, while six technicians operated the specialized tracking and timing equipment located in the forward fuselage. Accomodation in the rear included rest positions for the crew and nineteen seats for additional personnel. The maximum weight of the DC-7AMOR was 142,988lb and it had an endurance of twenty hours at 276.5mph.

The last DC-7C to be delivered (PH-DSR) went to KLM on 10 December 1958, by which time Boeing 707s were in service and the Douglas DC-8 jet was being tested. Nevertheless an attempt to take the DC-7C airframe into the jet-age as a potential competitor was made with the DC-7D project, a proposed DC-7C powered by four 5,800shp Rolls-Royce Tyne turboprops. But by then jet airliners, with their speed, comfort and economical operating costs, were making fast inroads into the airline market. Propeller-driven aircraft, even turboprops, were a dying breed in the long-haul market. Consequently the DC-7D project was abandoned, leaving the DC-7C last in a long line of Douglas piston-engined transports, which had proved their worth in war and peace, helped bring cheaper air travel to the people's of the world and pioneered a number of routes for the jetliners which followed.

One

Ancestry

A Douglas M-2 Mailplane (C150) of Western Air Express (WAE) in the 1920s with a 400hp Liberty. M-2s could carry two passengers, the front mail compartment being accessible via a forward cockpit opening and hatches. On 17 April 1926 the first M-2 mail flight left Salt Lake City for Los Angeles piloted by Charles James. Later that day the reverse run was made in another M-2 flown by Maury Graham. On May 23 the first two passengers were flown between Salt Lake City and Los Angeles in a WAE Douglas M-2 mailplane.

The first of thirty-seven Douglas O-38E observation biplanes ordered in 1933 for the USAAC. Based on the single O-38D, they differed in having a 625hp Pratt & Whitney Hornet engine, three-blade propeller, standard armament and opening rear canopy.

Operated by the 113th Observation Squadron, Indiana National Guard, this Douglas O-38E has had its cockpit canopy removed and is fitted with twin Edo floats. Note the number 5 marked on the fin and 'FIRST 11' on the fuselage .

Powered by two 450hp Pratt & Whitney Wasps, this amphibious Douglas Dolphin 129 was the second of two (NC14239/NC14240) delivered to Pan American Airways in 1934 for its subsidiary China National Aviation Corporation (CNAC). The two Dolphins operated CNACs coastal service, Route No.3, between Shanghai and Canton via Wenchow, Foochow, Amoy and Swatow for several years. In fact this pair (c/ns 1348 and 1349) were the last Dolphins built by Douglas, a type which had been its first production commercial passenger-carrying transport.

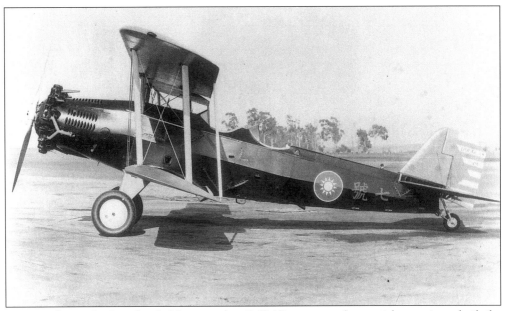

Very similar to the Douglas O-38 series, this O-2MC was one of over eighty variants built for the Chinese government between 1930 and 1936. Power is an uncowled 525hp Pratt & Whitney Hornet. It is seen here at Santa Monica prior to delivery.

The one-off 1931 Douglas XT3D torpedo-bomber (BuNo 8730) in updated 1933 form, with 800hp Twin Wasp engine, full NACA cowling, wheel spats and enclosed cockpits. With no orders placed the XT3D-2 was used as an engine test-bed and later at Norfolk NAS, Virginia, for instructional purposes.

An 0-35 observation monoplane, two 600hp Curtiss Conqueror engines, serving as a mailplane during the 1934 US Air Mail Crisis. Here USAAC O-35 No.6 was operating Air Mail Route 18, a Western Zone covering an area west of Cheyenne and Wyoming to the Pacific coast.

Following development of the Douglas YlO-31 and YO-43, the US Army ordered twenty-four O-43A observation monoplanes. Seen here is the first production O-43A (33-268) of 1934 powered by a 675hp Curtiss V-1570-59 in-line engine.

The prototype Douglas DC-1 during its first flight from Santa Monica on 1 July 1933. It carries the experimental registration X223Y and TWA colours. Powered by two 690hp Wright SGR-1820-F Cyclones it was progenitor of the DC-2 which followed and the famous DC-3 Dakota.

Douglas DC-2-120 NC14278, the fourth of sixteen ordered by American Airlines in 1934. In reality a 'stretched' version of the DC-1 with uprated Cyclone engines, the DC-2 was able to carry 14 passengers and became popular with a number of international airlines and the USAAC (C-32/-33/-39 series).

Famous name, famous plane. Donald W Douglas (centre) with K.D. Parmentier and J.J. Moll, crew of the KLM DC-2 (PH-AJU) standing behind. Named *Uiver*, it carried race number 44 and came second in overall speed, but first in the transport class when it participated in the Mac Robertson race from England to Australia in October 1934. It carried three passengers and mail, covering 11,123 miles from Mildenhall to Melbourne in 90.17 hours. This was an outstanding achievement as the DC-2 had raced against the De Havilland 88 Comet racer.

A direct development of the O-43A, this O-46A was one of ninety ordered from Douglas for the USAAC and Air National Guard. It differed from the O-43A in having a 725hp Pratt & Whitney R-1535-7 Twin Wasp Junior radial, a rear canopy faired into the fin and parallel struts between the wing and fuselage.

Competing against Consolidated's XP3Y-1 flying-boat in 1935 was the Douglas XP3D-1 seen here. With two 825hp Twin Wasps it first flew on 6 February 1935 and performed as well as the XP3Y-1. But US Navy choice fell on Consolidated's XP3Y-1 simply because each was $20,000 cheaper than an XP3D-1.

A Douglas TBD-1 Devastator torpedo-bomber (BuNo 0322) coded 6-T-1 with USN Squadron VT-6, c.1938-1939. TBD-ls were the Navy's first monoplane torpedo-bombers, had folding wings and a 900hp Twin Wasp engine. The type suffered heavy losses later at Midway and was thereafter used for training.

A bomber development of the DC-2 transport emerged as the B-18 Bolo. These two B-18As of the USAAC have a revised nose and 1,000hp Wright Cyclones. Many remained in service until 1942, after which they became B-18B anti-submarine aircraft equipped with magnetic airborne detection (MAD).

Probably the most famous passenger and military transport of all time, the Douglas DC-3 Dakota (USAAF C-47 Skytrain). In this shot is DC-3A-408 (NC30000) retained by Douglas for its own use. Engines are 1,200hp Pratt & Whitney Twin Wasps. No less than 10,654 DC-3s and variants were built by Douglas.

Donald W. Douglas is standing eighth from left in this picture of Douglas and American Airlines personnel. The DC-3 behind is NC25684 powered by 1,200hp Wright SGR-1820G-2 Cyclones. Built in May 1940 it became American Airlines DC-3 flagship.

Douglas hoped to interest Pan American Airways in its 1936 DF flying-boat with two 1,000hp Wright Cyclones. But PanAm did not want twin-engined flying-boats and the four built went to Japan and Russia. This Russian DF-151 (CCCP-H205) was used by Aeroflot on its Leningrad-Sevastopol route.

After Northrop became the E1 Segundo Division of Douglas in 1937 several Northrop designs were taken over by Douglas. This XBT-1 prototype (BuNo 9745) had made its first flight in August 1935 and introduced the perforated flaps which later featured on the Douglas Dauntless dive-bomber.

With an 825hp Twin Wasp Junior, Northrop XBT-2 (BuNu 0627), a BT-1 with retractable landing gear from the El Segundo plant, retained the perforated wing flaps and became the immediate forerunner of the Douglas SBD Dauntless.

Destined to earn fame in the Pacific War, the Douglas SBD Dauntless dive-bomber had a 1,000hp Wright Cyclone engine. It featured the perforated flaps used earlier on Northrop's XBT-1/-2 designs. This Dauntless SBD-1 (BuNo 1625) is with US Marine Squadron VMB-2 in 1940.

Equivalent to the Navy's SBD-4 Dauntless was the A-24A for the USAAF. They featured Army instrumentation and wireless equipment and a pneumatic tyre for the tailwheel replaced the Navy SBD solid type. This unmarked A-24A is believed to be on a delivery flight from Douglas to the USAAF in 1942.

Built by Douglas at El Segundo (formerly Northrop) was this export version of the A-17A attack bomber. One of ten built for Peru as a Douglas 8A-3P its engine was a 1,000hp Wright Cyclone. These 8A-3Ps were used in Peru's 1941 war against Ecuador and the last not withdrawn until the late 1950s.

Destined for the French Armée de l'Aire an early Douglas DB-7 awaits despatch from El Segundo where it was built. Engines were 1,000hp Pratt & Whitney Twin Wasps. Armament included four forward-firing fuselage guns plus one each in dorsal and ventral positions. The maximum bomb load was 1,764lb.

Night Intruder version of the RAF Douglas Boston II was the Havoc I with nose glazing and four machine-guns mounted under the nose. This matt black (night finish) Havoc I seen in 1940 was BD112/'YP-T' of 23 Squadron RAF.

A busy scene at the Douglas Santa Monica plant in around 1939-1940, with over thirty DB-7Bs and A-20 attack bombers scheduled for RAF and USAAC service respectively. Also nearing completion are two DC-3s for American Airlines. Notice that the two A-20s nearest camera (Nos 147/149) are awaiting the fitting of their outer wing panels. The RAF machines would become Douglas Boston IIIs and operate in the European, Middle Eastern and Italian war zones. The RAF Boston III Intruder carried an under-fuselage gun pack housing four 20-mm cannon. A number of Boston IIIs went to the RCAF (Canada), RAAF (Australia), SAAF (South Africa) and Soviet Air Force.

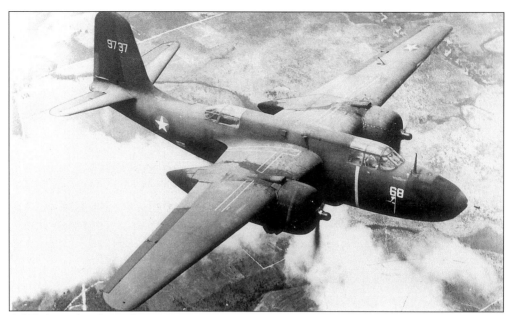

A US Army Air Corps decision to convert sixty A-20s to night fighter configuration resulted in the P-70 with 1,600hp Wright Cyclone 14 engines, British AI Mk IV radar, deletion of bomb racks and defensive armament and fitting of a belly gun pack mounting four 20-mm cannon. This USAAC P-70 (No 68) is serialled 39-0737 (9737).

In 1941 an Army A-20A was evaluated by the Navy as a BD-1 (BuNo 4251). Eight more followed in 1942 as BD-2s (BuNos 7035-7042)being A-20B conversions. They were used by the Marine Corps for target towing and general duties. One of the BD-2s is pictured here.

Most proliferous of the A-20 series was the A-20G with four nose-mounted guns, a total of 2,850 being built. Designated A-20G-20, the USAAF machine seen here (42-86573) carries a 374 US gallon drop tank under the fuselage. Its engines were 1,600hp Wright R-2600-23s. This picture dates from around 1943-1944.

Due to heavy military demands only twelve Douglas DC-5s were built. A sixteen-seat transport five went to the civil market and seven to the US Navy and Marine Corps) as R3D-1s and R3D-2s. DC-5s flew with KLM on its West Indies and Netherlands East Indies routes. Power was provided by a pair of 900hp Wright Cyclones. Three R3D-2s were still with the USMC in 1946.

A civil conversion of a 1939 Douglas B-23 Dragon bomber with 1,600hp Wright Cyclones. Original armament was four-guns one each in nose, dorsal, ventral and tail positions. Max bomb load 2,000lb. Quickly superseded in USAAC service, some B-23s (thirty-eight were built) became civil transports like N747 seen here.

Douglas began work on the giant B-19 bomber in 1935 to USAAC requirements. Powered by four 2,000hp Wright Duplex Cyclones first flight was on 27 June 1941. Armament included sixteen guns and a maximum bomb load of 37,100lb. The plane was used as a transport in the Second World War with Allison in-line engines but only one was built.

Two
The DC-4E Mainliner

A joint venture involving Douglas Aircraft, United, American and Eastern Airlines resulted in the DC-4E (E=experimental) airliner. The one and only prototype (NX18100), powered by four 1,450hp Pratt & Whitney Twin Hornets, is seen here on finals. Named 'Super Mainliner' it went to United Airlines for a number of proving flights on their network. Handling results were pleasing, but performance was disappointing and the aircraft too complex. Further development was therefore suspended in favour of a less sophisticated layout which was to emerge as the DC-4A and C-54.

In this picture the massive proportions of the Douglas DC-4E tail unit are apparent. The centre fin is integral to the fuselage, while outer fins and rudders are mounted at the extreme tips of the tailplane which has noticeable dihedral. The use of a nosewheel (first on an aircraft of this size) necessitated the high steps to provide passengers access via the rear port entry door. The DC-4E carried forty-two passengers by day, or thirty at night with full sleeping facilities including a private bridal suite.

Fine in-flight study of the Douglas DC-4E airliner of 1938, which first flew from Clover Field, Santa Monica, on 7 June that year. The wings, with tapered leading-edges, contained three spars and the inward-retracting main landing gear with one wheel to each leg.

This unmarked Douglas DC-4, smaller and less complex than its DC-4E progenitor, is shown here to emphasise the external changes: tapered leading and trailing wing edges, single fin and rudder, no tailplane dihedral, a smaller fuselage and a revised cockpit and nose layout.

15335   DC-4   6-20-39

An historic occasion this, as Douglas DC-4E 'Super Mainliner' was handed over to United Airlines for its proving flights with that company. Technically advanced in design, the DC-4E had slotted wing flaps, innovatory power-boosted controls, an auxiliary power system comprising two small engines, AC electrical system and air conditioned cabin. It was intended production aircraft would be fully pressurised. On the lower step is Donald W. Douglas himself, with Douglas personnel and United Airlines staff included in the party. Note the piper and the chef alongside Donald Douglas.

Three
The Skymaster Series

Arrangements for a night flight are shown in this Douglas cutaway of the original DC-4 layout. Similar in concept to the DC-4E, it was a new design lighter and less complex in construction. It had a fuselage of circular cross-section smaller than its predecessor, wings of less area with higher aspect-ratio and tapered leading and trailing edges, twin main wheels fitted to a landing gear which retracted forward and up into the inner engine nacelles, accomodation for forty day passengers or twenty-eight by night, and a choice of either four 1,000hp Wright Cyclone or four 1,050hp Pratt & Whitney Twin Wasp engines. The new aircraft was designated DC-4A.

With the Japanese attack on Pearl Harbor, USAAC took over the Douglas DC-4A production line at Santa Monica and all became C-54 or C-54A military transports. This USAAC C-54 Skymaster is in the familiar olive drab and grey finish of US Army Air Corps machines, c.1942.

Here a C-54B Skymaster is moved via the overhead hoist at the Douglas Santa Monica plant during the Second World War. The machine under construction below is a C-54E. Note the riveting details, rear engine nacelle mounting to wing, the wing rib structure and the aerofoil section.

In September 1944 a USAAF C-54A Skymaster (42-107465) leaves Prestwick, Scotland, with US-bound American wounded from the European theatre. Note the metal finish and the B-24 Liberator and two B-25 Mitchells in the background.

Rear fuselage and tail unit assembly of a C-54 Skymaster at Santa Monica during the Second World War. The circular fuselage section, fin and rudder details, tailplane join and riveting system are clearly seen in this picture.

A profusion of C-54 Skymasters and DC-3s outside the Douglas Santa Monica plant in 1944. The Californian sun obviously allowed these kinds of final stages in production. Notice the line of completed DC-3s in front of the main building.

In this picture, taken some time after the war, this Douglas C-54E Skymaster wears USAF colours and was in service with the Air National Guard (ANG), Connecticut, with that unit's crest on the fin. Engines were four 1,350hp Pratt & Whitney R-2000 Twin Wasps.

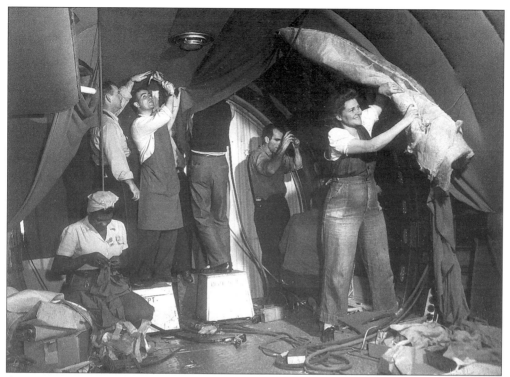

A post-war scene at the Douglas plant as workers proceed to convert an ex-military C-54 Skymaster to civil DC-4 standard by installing more luxurious and soundproof surroundings. A majority of post-war civil DC-4s were ex-military machines converted to airliner standards.

Brand new Douglas DC-4-1009 airliner under construction in 1946 at Santa Monica for Mexican National Airlines. The C-54 up front is being converted to DC-4 standard for American Air Express. Notice the lowered flaps on the nearest aircraft.

In 1946 Donald W. Douglas stands beside a DC-4 at the Santa Monica plant, a time when numerous ex-military C-54s were being converted at the site to DC-4 standard and newly built DC-4-1009s nearing completion for airline customers.

An ex-military C-54 Skymaster which has been converted to civil DC-4 standard and registered NC41007. It is seen here in service during the 1950s with Hawaiian Airlines powered by four 1,450hp Pratt & Whitney Twin Wasp engines.

Watch out for planes! An unidentified road/runway perimeter crossing in Belgium, with one of Sabena airline's DC-4-1009s (OO-CBQ) creating interest for some of the local populace as it taxies past *en route* for its take-off point.

This interior of a Douglas DC-4 shows to what extent a sense of luxury could be achieved by converting the many military C-54s which became available after the war. This appears to be one of those company sponsored publicity photographs in which seated passengers adopt selected poses.

In its element with four Pratt & Whitney Twin Wasps in full cry is American Airlines DC-4 flagship NC90417 *Monterrey*. This was another ex-USAAF C-54 Skymaster converted to civil DC-4 standard by Douglas at Santa Monica.

The Australian airline Qantas became a regular user of the DC-4, in this case it is an ex-USAAF C-54B conversion with 1,350hp (1,100hp at 7,00Oft) Pratt & Whitney R-2000-3 radial engines. Registered VH-EBM it flew on Qantas international routes. Note the Australian flag and the name on the fin.

With registration ZS-BMH this DC-4-1009 for South African Airways was the last DC-4 built. With four 1,450hp Twin Wasps it is seen leaving Santa Monica on its delivery flight.

Visiting Blackbushe UK in 1959 was this ex-military C-54 Skymaster converted to DC-4 configuration. Registered as N88939 it was serving with American International Airlines.

Skymasters spread their wings far and wide. This ex-USAAF C-54 civil conversion is seen when operating as LV-AGG with Aerolineas Argentinas in the 1950s.

Scandinavian Airlines System (SAS) used quite a number of Skymasters. This ex-military C-54 conversion to DC-4 is registered LN-IAD (Norway) and named *Haakon Viking*. It is seen at Northolt in the 1950s.

On finals here is another ex-USAAF C-54 in service with KLM (Royal Dutch Airlines). Registered PH-TAG it is in overall metal finish and early KLM colour scheme. Note the last two letters of registration (AG) marked at the top of the fin.

After serving with major airlines, many DC-4s were sold to secondary companies. This ex-military C-54 (N30048) has been acquired by the American based Seven Seas Airlines. Note the Neptune tri-pronged fork logo on fin and rudder.

In 1952 Japan Air Lines (JAL) was allowed to operate its own aircraft with Japanese crews. They began with two DC-4s (ex-military C-54s) and started a Tokyo-San Francisco service. Here JAL DC-4, JA6012, is at Tokyo airport in the 1950s.

Smartly turned-out and photographed at Blackbushe Airport UK in 1959 was this Douglas C-54/DC-4, G-APTT, of Trans Arabia Airways. Four Pratt & Whitney R-2000-7 Twin Wasp engines.

South and Central America was a happy hunting ground for the C-54/DC-4 Skymaster. Here, in the mid-1950s, TG-ADA of Aviateca Guatemala is about to start up its Pratt & Whitney Twin Wasps. Note the name *Tikal* marked beneath the cockpit window.

The C-54 Skymaster made a very useful freight carrier and as such was flown by a number of civil operators. Here VH-INX of Ansett-ANA, Australia, is seen in 1968 operating as a freighter, named across the fin and rudder 'Cargomaster'.

In the white, blue, grey livery of Air France, a C-54/DC-4 (F-BELH) prepares for its next flight in the mid-1950s. By then the airline was serving the French Colonies, flying trans-Atlantic services and expanding its Far East network.

Based in the Pacific and flying domestic and international routes, this C-54/DC-4 with four Pratt & Whitney R-2000-3 Twin Wasps belongs to Polynesian Airlines. The legend below the pilot's window reads: 'Super Skymaster SANDA'.

On the British civil register as G-ALEP in 1949 was this ex-military C-54 Skymaster, four Pratt & Whitney R-2000-3 Twin Wasps and an overall metal finish. At the time it was owned by Mining and Exploration Air Services Ltd. Note the tripod style of ground tail support.

Another of Australia's Ansett-ANA C-54 freighters, VH-ANF. In this case the large freight doors just aft of the wing root can be clearly defined, as can the name 'Cargomaster' across the fin and rudder.

This 1959 shot is of a Saudi Arabian Airlines C-54/DC-4, Skymaster, HZ-AAW, its four Pratt & Whitney R-2000 Twin Wasps patiently waiting their next trip. The aircraft was visiting Blackbushe aerodrome UK.

An unusual visitor to the UK in the early 1960s was this C-54/DC-4 Skymaster, VQ-ZEC, when operated by Bechuanaland National Airways. The four-engined transport at the rear is a Dutch-registered de Havilland DH 114 Heron. Note the earlier style of Shell and BP aviation fuel bowsers.

Military use of the C-54 Skymaster continued for some years after the Second World War. Here a USAAF Douglas Chicago-built C-54D (42-72505/'B') named *Bee Liner* is in transit at Itazuke Air Force Base, Japan, at the end of the Korean War in 1953. Its engines were 1,350hp Pratt & Whitney R-2000-11 Twin Wasps.

The USAAF transferred eighty-six C-54D Skymasters to the US Navy as R5D-3s (they became C-54Qs in 1962). In service here with the US Navy's Air Transport Service (NATS) in the 1960s is a C-54Q, BuNo 56528, with Pratt & Whitney R-2000-11 Twin Wasps.

Many C-54s ended up with foreign air forces, like this C-54D No T3-17 of the Spanish Air Force, '353-27' of Esc 353, a transport unit. This picture was taken in 1972.

An unusual visitor to Blackbushe aerodrome, UK, in around 1958-1959 was this US Marine Corps Douglas R5D-3 (BuNo 56484)/'CZ' one of eighty-six ex-USAAF C-54Ds transferred to US Navy/Marine service.

Most numerous of the Skymaster series was the C-54D, of which 380 were built, all at the Douglas Chicago plant, with 1,350hp Pratt & Whitney R-2000-11 Twin Wasps. This 1962 shot is of C-54D, 45-0544, of the US Air Force Communications Service (AFCS) as shown on the fuselage, fin and rudder.

Another Skymaster still in military service during 1970 was this C-54D (7503) of the Portuguese Air Force. On finals here with flaps lowered and Pratt & Whitney R-2000-11 Twin Wasps throttled back for touch down.

In full camouflage finish this C-54 Skymaster was still in service with the South African Air Force (SAAF) in 1981. It is numbered 6904 and operated with No.44 Squadron, SAAF, powered by Pratt & Whitney R-2000 Twin Wasp engines.

The large freight loading doors are apparent in this 1960s view of a C-54 Skymaster in service with the Royal Danish Air Force, serial number N-706. Four 1,450hp Pratt & Whitney R-2000-4 engines provided the power.

Another European air arm which employed the Skymaster was the Belgian Air Force. This 1970 picture shows one of its C-54s, OT-CWV/'KX2', from No.15 Wing. Power was provided by four 1,350hp Pratt & Whitney Twin Wasps.

The USAF Military Air Transport Service (MATS) received 38 C-54Ds (later HC-54D) modified by Convair as SC-54Ds for its Air Rescue service. Special radar gear and rear observation blisters were fitted. This was 42-72601 of MATS No.67 ARS.

Modified fuel tank arrangements and rapid cargo to trooper conversion resulted in the C-54E. This example seen in 1968 was USAF No.44-9041, in service with the Hawaii Air National Guard and named *Spirit of Aloha*.

Powered by four 1,450hp Pratt & Whitney R-2000-9 Twin Wasps, this R5D-5 (later C-54S) was a naval version of the C-54G of which some thirteen were allocated to the US Coast Guard. One of these (5614) is seen at Prestwick, Scotland, in the 1960s.

Fitted with special meteorological observation equipment, this WC-54D (42-72618), originally a C-54D, was issued to the USAF/MATS Weather Center in the 1960s. Note the weather logo spread across the fin and rudder.

With its inner Twin Wasp engines in taxiing mode, a US Navy Douglas R5D-3 (later C-54Q), an ex-USAF C-54D, trundles past the camera. BuNo 56521/'JM', it displays Navy Squadron's VR-24 number on the fuselage. Beneath the cockpit is written 'Ciudad Madrid'.

Undergoing heavy maintenance here in 1963 is C-54 Skymaster, TF-SIF, of the Icelandic Coast Guard. It would appear the starboard wing tip has also been damaged and awaits repair.

One of two C-54 Skymasters which flew with the Fuerza Aerea Guatemalteca (the Guatemalan Air Force), this machine was delivered on 28 May 1975 and numbered 800. It flew with the FAG until February 1980 when it was written off.

Some C-54/DC-4s arrived in Great Britain. This C-54B/DC-4 (ex-USAAF No.43-17133) is registered G-APNH here and in service with Air Charter London around 1958/59. It was later converted by Aviation Traders to Carvair configuration.

A C-54E (ex-USAAF 42-72232) as UK registered G-ASPN and with Invicta Air Cargo around 1970. It had first gone to the US Navy (BuNo 39175), became NC49288 in the US, sold as AP-ADL in Pakistan, back to US as N49288, to Saudi Arabia (HZ-AAG), then UK and finally South Africa in 1972 as ZS-IRE.

London Heathrow was the venue here in the 1960s for this C-54/DC-4 of the Spanish airline Trans Europa, taxiing past using all four Pratt & Whitney Twin Wasp engines. The registration is EC-BDK and on the rear fuselage is written 'Compañia de Aviación'.

Thousands of miles of hostile jungle faced many transport aircraft on South America's domestic routes. Here a C-54 (HK2377) of Colombia's Aero Transportes Amazonas (ATA) awaits its next duty in 1982.

The Venezuelan airline Linea Expresa Bolivar CA (LEBCA) was founded in 1958 and lasted just ten years. It used several types of aircraft, including this C-54 Skymaster registered YV-C-LBM. It is pictured here in 1965.

Noted for its conveyance of fresh beef products by air was the Bolivian carrier Fri Reyes. Here one of their C-54s (CP1206) waits for its next assignment in the 1960s.

As C-54/DC-4 Skymasters were replaced by more modern types of aircraft, many went to secondary airlines or air freight carriers. In this 1978 photo the large cargo loading doors are clearly seen on 9Q-CAQ, a C-54 operating with Transair Cargo of Zaire.

Four

The ATL 98 Carvair

When Channel Air Bridge Ltd wanted a replacement for their Bristol 32 Freighter car ferries in 1959, they selected a conversion of the Douglas DC-4 Skymaster. It was reliable, becoming redundant as a major airliner, cheap and with a vast spares back-up. The resulting Aviation Traders Ltd 98 Carvair proved ideal, with its redesigned bulbous nose 8ft 8in longer than a DC-4, the flight deck raised 6ft 10in and the nosewheel retracting into an external fairing. Vehicular entry was via a platform and sideways swinging nose door worked hydraulically. The Carvair accomodated five cars and twenty-three passengers. This late 1960s shot is of Carvair G-ASDC *Big Louie* of British Air Ferries. Note the front nose section which is swung open.

LX-IOF, an ex-Interocean (Luxembourg) DC-4, in the process of conversion to ATL Carvair configuration at Stansted late in 1959. The seventeenth Carvair produced, LX-IOF (re-registered as G-AXAI) remained at Stansted until March 1969 when it went to CIE Air Transport.

In overall white finish and carrying International Red Cross markings, this Douglas/ATL 98 Carvair is registered as LN-NAA of Norway in the early 1970s. Engines are four 1,450hp Pratt & Whitney R-2000-7M2 Twin Wasps. The external fairing for the nosewheel to retract into is clearly seen.

Ideal for heavy and bulky loads, the Douglas/ATL 98 Carvair was used in its later years by several international air freighting organisations. Here US-registered N89FA wears the large, striped insignia of Falcon Airways Cargo. Note the starboard flap in its lowered position.

Originating as UK registered G-ATRV and making its initial flight on 25 March 1966, this Douglas/ATL 98 Carvair went later to the Lebanon as OD-ADW, passed to British United Air Ferries and was disposed of to France as F-BOSU, where it flew with CIE Air Transport as seen here in the 1970s.

First flown on 27 October 1965 this ATL 98 Carvair was built as VH-INK for the Australian airline Ansett-ANA to be used on their cargo routes. The large loading doors in the rear port fuselage can be seen clearly. Note the name Carvair below the cockpit and across the upper fin and rudder.

Originally registered N9757F and first flown on 2 November 1962, this ATL 98 Carvair became UK-registered G-AREK, but was sold later to Interocean cargo carriers of Luxembourg and registered LX-IOH as depicted here. Notice that only the smaller portion of the rear port loading door is open.

Five

The Canadair
North Star

A Rolls-Royce Merlin-powered Douglas DC-4 was produced by Canadair Ltd at Montreal, Canada. As the C-54 GM North Star a number of unpressurized aircraft with four 1,160hp Rolls-Royce Merlin 620s or 1,420hp Merlin 622s went to the Royal Canadian Air Force (RCAF). Trans-Canada Airlines ordered twenty pressurized DC-4M-2/3s (Merlin 622s) or DC-4M-2/4s driving three-blade or four-blade propellers respectively. British Overseas Airways Corporation (BOAC) ordered twenty-two pressurized Canadair C-4s with 1,760hp Merlin 626s and called them the Argonaut class. They operated BOAC's international routes until 1958 when they were disposed of to other airlines. Here, in around 1959-1960, a BOAC C-4 (G-ALHR *Antiope*) has been sold to Aden Airways and will be re-registered VR-AAR.

Similar to the British C-4 Argonaut class was the C-4-1 which differed only in minor details. The last of four for Canadian Pacific Airlines, this was CF-CPP named *Empress of Hong Kong*, powered by Rolls-Royce Merlin 626 engines. It was delivered to CPA in July 1949.

The only Canadian-built DC-4 variant to have radial engines was this C-5 built in 1950 as a VIP and/or long-range crew trainer for the RCAF. Four 2,100hp Pratt & Whitney R-2800-CA15 radials provided the power, and it flew with No 412 Squadron, RCAF, serial 17524 (later 10000). It was withdrawn in 1967.

Pictured in 1966, this Canadair DC-4M-2 with Merlin 622s (three-blade propellers) belonged to the Canadian National Aeronautical Establishment. Registered CF-SVP-X it was used on experimental and research duties. Note the extended rear fuselage apparently containing magnetic anomaly detection equipment (MAD).

With its four 1,760hp Rolls-Royce Merlin 626s in full cry a BOAC Canadair C-4 is in its element. One of the Argonaut class its registration is G-ALHX and the name, marked beneath the cockpit window, is *Astraea*. The last of the BOAC Argonaut class was withdrawn in April 1960.

Good view of the annular radiators fitted to the Merlin 626 engines of Canadair C-4s. In service here during 1960 with Overseas Aviation Ltd of Southend is G-ALHN, originally a BOAC Argonaut class named *Argosy*.

Canadair C-4 G-ALHS of Derby Airways is shown some time between 1961 and 1964. This aircraft originated as BOAC Argonaut class *Astra* in 1949 passing to Overseas Aviation Ltd in 1960. It then went to Derby Airways as seen here before going to British Midland Airways in December 1964. It was scrapped in 1970.

Six

The DC-6 Series

Although an updated DC-4 Skymaster was planned during the Second World War and complied with USAAF requirements under military designation XC-112, initial orders for a civil version for when peace came were placed as early as 1944. American Airlines signed for fifty followed by United Airlines with twenty. Designated DC-6, the revised design was essentially a DC-4 with more powerful R-2800 Double Wasp engines, a fuselage 'stretch' of 6ft 11in providing accomodation for a further ten passengers, and full cabin pressurization which enabled flying at fuel-economical high altitude. The first DC-6 flight was in June 1946, with deliveries to American and United Airlines following that November. DC-6s were introduced to United Airline's transcontinental service on 27 April 1947. This official Douglas cutaway shows the general seating arrangements and cabin layout for a DC-6.

One from a batch of ten DC-6s for Scandinavian Airlines System (SAS) of Sweden registered SE-BDA to SE-BDI, this DC-6 (SE-BDG) is on a Douglas company test flight over its home state of California in the early 1950s. Engines were four 2,400hp Pratt & Whitney R-2800-CB16 Twin Wasps.

An official Douglas publicity photograph showing the interior seating arrangements and decor in the forward port side of a DC-6. Note the square windows (C-54/DC-4s had an oval type), curtains, the partition to the galley and that two front seats are facing backwards.

The first overseas airline to operate the Douglas DC-6, Sabena of Belgium, initially acquired five for its international routes from Brussels to New York and the Belgian Congo. In this photograph, taken on 3 March 1953 at Melsbrock, is Sabena's DC-6 OO-SDE.

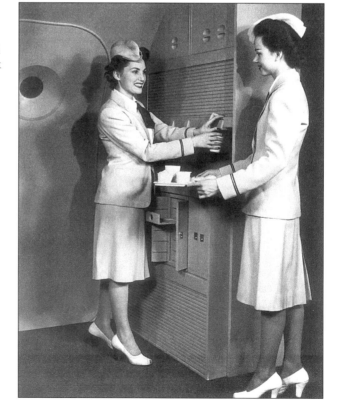

Obviously posed for as part of a Douglas promotional, this photograph shows two airline stewardesses preparing drinks and snacks from the galley of a DC-6. Notice the compactness of the cupboards and small drawers.

Powered by four 2,400hp Pratt & Whitney R-2800-CB16 Twin Wasps, this DC-6 PH-TPB *Prince Bernhard* was one from a second batch built for KLM (Royal Dutch Airlines). It is being prepared for its next scheduled flight from Schipol International Airport, Amsterdam, in the 1950s.

Conversion arrangements for overnight travel comprising two-tier bunks provided in the separate ladies lounge on board a Douglas DC-6 airliner.

Passengers boarding a KLM (Royal Dutch Airlines) Douglas DC-6 with its fuselage legend 'The Flying Dutchman'. This machine, PH-DPI, carries the name *Prinses Irene* on its nose below the cockpit.

Photographed in 1949, this Douglas DC-6, PI-C 292, was newly built for Philippine Air Lines (PAL) and carries the name *Lingayen* on its nose. Powered by four 2,100hp Pratt & Whitney R-2800-CA15 Twin Wasp engines, it flew PAL's international routes.

Pictured at London, Heathrow, in the late 1950s is an Air France Douglas DC-6. Its four-blade paddle-type propellers indicate 2,400hp R-2800-CB16 Twin Wasps. Note the two BEA Viscount 802s (G-AOHO on left and G-AOHU) in background and the Hunting Clan buildings in the distance.

With its four Pratt & Whitney R-2800 Twin Wasps throttled back, Delta Airlines DC-6 N1906M, Fleet No.606, follows the ground handler's directions to its dispersal point. It is interesting to see how Delta has its name applied to the engine cowlings as well as the fuselage, fin and rudder.

Military use was also made of the Douglas DC-6 in some air arms. Here on finals, with everything down, is 31-8 of the Aeronautica Militare Italiana. At this time in the 1960s it was operating with 302° Gruppo (RVSM). The R-2800 Twin Wasps are driving three-blade paddle-type propellers.

The starboard pair of three-blade paddle-type propellers, driven by 2,400hp Pratt & Whitney R-2800-CB16 Twin Wasps, appear to be 'feathered' on this Belgian Air Force DC-6. Coded OT-CDA/'KY-I', it was photographed in 1971 when operating with FAB, 15 SML.

Pictured in 1962, a Douglas DC-6 of the Royal New Zealand Air Force (RNZAF). Powered by four 2,400hp Pratt & Whitney R-2800-CB16 Twin Wasps, this machine, NZ3631, was serving at the time with No.40 Squadron. It has the three-blade paddle-type fully reversible propellers fitted.

With four R-2800-CB16 Twin Wasps and a revised interior, this DC-6 (NX90809) is on a test flight from Santa Monica prior to having its C of A issued (hence the NX prefix). In DC-6A freighter configuration it was later delivered to Slick Airways as N90809 together with two other DC-6As, N90810 and N90811.

When Pratt & Whitney introduced their more powerful R-2800 Twin Wasp radial with water/methanol injection in 1948, it persuaded Douglas another 5ft stretch was possible in the DC-6 airframe. This resulted in the DC-6A Liftmaster, an all-cargo variant with blanked-off windows, 2,400hp R-2800-CB16 engines driving paddle-blade propellers and a maximum 107,000lb take-off weight of which 33,027lb was payload. The initial flight of the DC-6A was on 29 September 1949, the last of seventy-four built being delivered in 1959. Here, exhibiting its advantages, is the original Douglas-owned DC-6A Liftmaster (N30006) showing the large fore and aft freight loading doors and paddle-blade propellers.

Loading at Amsterdam, a Dutch KLM Douglas DC-6A, PH-TGA. Aft of the crew entry door is the aircraft's name, *DR. IR. M.H. Damme*. This view shows clearly the engine cowling gills open and the paddle-type propeller blades.

With 2,500hp R-2800-CB17 Double Wasps driving three-blade fully reversible propellers, this DC-6A No 63 of France's Aeronavale in the 1970s originally operated with Canadian Pacific Airlines as CF-CUS.

The military equivalent to the DC-6A was the C-118 which flew with the USAF (C-118A) and US Navy (C-118B). Here visiting a Mildenhall Air Show on 9 October 1984 is a US Navy C-118B (BuNo 131578) which had flown in from the naval station at Keflavik, Iceland, where it was based.

Pictured here in 1956 is a Douglas DC-6A belonging to Slick Airways, which specialized in freight transport. Its registration was N6814C and power was provided by Pratt & Whitney engines, either the 2,400hp R-2800-CB16s or the 2,500hp CB17s.

Nice close-up of a Belgian Sabena airlines DC-6A, OO-CTO, revving up its four Pratt & Whitney R-2800-CB16 or CB17 engines, the wheel chocks still in position. This shot shows to advantage the style of nose-wheel and doors.

Some of the major airlines operated Douglas DC-6As on their freight services. This is DC-6A N6258C *Clipper Gladiator* of Pan American World Airways clipper cargo. It had four Pratt & Whitney R-2800-CB16 or CB17 engines rated at 2,400 or 2,500hp respectively.

Douglas produced a very successful passenger update of the DC-6 in parallel with the DC-6A freighter. Designated DC-6B it did not have the reinforced floor and large cargo doors of the DC-6A. Accomodation was provided initially for fifty-four passengers, but 102 could be carried in high-density form. The DC-6B was powered by either 2,400hp R-2800-CB16, or 2,500hp R-2800-CB17 Twin Wasps. The initial flight of the DC-6B was on 2 February 1951 and the first scheduled operator, American Airlines, introduced DC-6Bs on its transcontinental route on 29 April 1951. This DC-6B (N572) shows off its pristine condition and Northwest Airline colours.

The most produced version of the DC-6 was the DC-6B, of which 286 were built. Airborne here during the 1950s, with 2,500hp R-2800-CB17s driving three-blade fully reversible propellers, is DC-6B N6528C *Clipper Midnight Sun* of Pan American World Airways.

Seen here on 31 May 1955 (location unknown) is OO-CTH, a Douglas DC-6B of Belgium's national airline Sabena. It has 2,500hp Pratt & Whitney R-2800-CB17 engines driving three-blade paddle-type propellers. In the distance are three DC-3s, one a USAF C-47, and four USAF Fairchild C-119 transports which appear to be in Arctic markings.

Taxiing out to its take-off point at Amsterdam's Schipol Airport in the 1950s is DC-6B PH-TFK (originally PH-DFK) of KLM Royal Dutch Airlines. This 'Flying Dutchman' carries the name *Jan Huyghen Van Linschoten* on the fuselage side.

From 1946 onwards Scandinavian Airlines System (SAS) relied heavily on Douglas airliners for its long-haul routes. Here a Danish-registered DC-6B, OY-?? *Torkil Viking*, shows off its fully reversible paddle-blade propellers, each driven by a 2,500hp Pratt & Whitney R-2800-CB17 radial.

Another Scandinavia-based airline was Sterling Airways of Sweden, which also flew Douglas types. This was SE-ENY, one of their DC-6Bs with R-2800-CB17 engines and three-blade fully reversible propellers. Note the baggage train under the rear fuselage and the stewardess awaiting passengers in the doorway.

Being prepared for its next flight in the summer of 1967 is a Douglas DC-6B of the Belgian airline Sobelair. Registered OO-CTL, it has four R-2800-CB17 radials driving reversible paddle-blade propellers. The engine cooling gills are open.

Passengers at London Heathrow in 1961 boarding I-DIMA, a Douglas DC-6B of the Italian airline Societá Aerea Mediterranea (SAM). This has paddle-blade propellers fitted to its Pratt & Whitney R-2800-CB16 or CB17 engines.

On its landing approach, believed to be at London Airport in the early 1960s, a throttled-back Douglas DC-6B of Icelandair descends with everything down. Registered TF-FIP it carries below the logo on its fin the name *Flugfelag Islands*.

Basking in the sun in 1968 was this Douglas DC-6B of Syrian Arab Airlines (SAAL). With Pratt & Whitney R-2800-CB16 or CB17 engines it has the fully reversible three-blade paddle-type propellers. Registered YK-AEC it carries Syria's national flag marking on the fin.

Nearer its birthplace is this Douglas DC-6B of US-based Western Airlines. Registered N91307, its Western fleet number was 907-C. As it taxies past the camera the cooling gills on the R-2800-CB17 engines are partly open. Note Western's Indian head motif and the following cheat line.

A 1963 photograph of YU-AFF, a Douglas DC-6B belonging to Adria Airways of Yugoslavia. It has fully-reversible three-blade propellers .

With fore and aft baggage doors open in the lowerfuselage, this Douglas DC-6B, OH-KDC of Kar Air, Finland, is pictured at Stansted, UK, in the 1960s. This machine is fitted with the paddle-type propeller blades and powered by R-2800-CB16 or CB17 engines.

Pictured here on 11 June 1979 at Le Bourget is a Douglas DC-6B of UTA Industries/Securité Civile. Registered F-GAPK it was originally F-BGOC with TAI, then went to the Armée de l'Air as 43834/64-PI before going to UTA. It has a large freight pannier fitted beneath the centre-section.

Like other earlier Douglas transports, a number of DC-6Bs ended up in military service. This one, serving with the Portuguese Air Force in the late 1960s, is serialled 6710 and is seen here on a very wet day at London Heathrow.

Seven
The DC-7 Series

TWA was a serious threat to American Airlines in 1950 due to its Turbo-Compound-powered Super Constellations. Not to be beaten, American persuaded Douglas to produce an updated DC-6B fitted with the new Turbo-Compound engines. A promise of $40 million towards twenty-five of the revised aircraft assured Douglas of most development costs and work commenced on the DC-7. Another 40in fuselage stretch added an extra row of seats, DC-6B maximum tankage of 5,525 US gallons remained, titanium was used in engine nacelle construction to reduce fire risk, the landing gear was strengthened and designed to act as a brake if lowered at high speed in an emergency and power was provided by four 3,250hp Wright R-3350-18DA-2 Turbo-Compounds. Here the first DC-7 (N301AA) is on test in 1953 wearing Douglas colours. It later went to American Airlines who introduced the type on 29 November that year.

A busy Santa Monica assembly line in the early 1950s where Douglas DC-7 airliners are under construction. The centre machine, number 462, is the first for United Airlines and was registered N6301C. Altogether United received fifty-seven DC-7s, the last being registered N6357C.

A good idea of the constructional methods used at Douglas can be gathered from this detailed photograph from March 1953, as a DC-7 is about to have its fuselage and wings joined together. Note the overhead cranes and giant slings around the fore and aft fuselage sections.

An interior view looking aft along a Douglas DC-7 airliner's main passenger cabin. The decor, seating and space availability are luxurious compared to modern jet airliners. It is also interesting to see the pillows provided in apparent abundance on the overhead racks.

The flight deck of a Douglas DC-7 transport, showing to advantage the Captain and Flight Engineer's positions, with controls up front and, on the left, interphones, amplifiers, VHF transmitters and radio equipment.

Up where it belongs with four 3,250hp Wright R-3350-18DA-2 Turbo-Compound engines in full cry, this Douglas DC-7 was one of fifty-seven owned by American Airlines. Registered N303AA the lettering under the cockpit identifies it as the airline's *Flagship Missouri*.

Resplendent in Delta Airline's old dark blue and white colours is DC-7 N4876C, fleet number 706. Delta purchased ten DC-7s and late in the 1950s, together with a number of Convair 340s and 440s, they were the last piston-engined airliners to enter Delta service.

Looking forward along the cabin of a Douglas DC-7, this photograph shows clearly the kitchen/galley compartment with its food cupboards and row of drink dispensers. Notice the telephone and switch panel on the left of the little girl.

From a completely different angle, American Airlines DC-7 N303AA *Flagship Missouri* flies along an unidentified part of the United States coastline (believed to be California). This DC-7 (Douglas c/n 44125) was the third of its type to be acquired by American Airlines.

Passengers enjoy the comforts of a lounge-style rear end as incorporated into a Douglas DC-7 fuselage. Once again it is interesting to observe the luxury and space availability on these piston airliners when compared to even first class accomodation on today's jets.

Once again, American Airlines N303AA *Flagship Missouri* – on *terra firma* this time – is displayed for the camera. Here passengers leave the aircraft via its rear port doorway. Noteworthy is the airline's eagle motif between A-A and the streamlined step-trolley sporting the Douglas badge.

The prototype Douglas DC-7B, externally similar to the DC-7, but having lengthened engine nacelles incorporating saddle tanks to carry extra fuel. This particular aircraft (N70D) first flew in October 1954 and is shown in Douglas colours. After certification it went to Delta Air Lines as a DC-7.

Powered by four 3,250hp Wright R-3350-18DA-4 Turbo-Compound engines, this DC-7B (N777PA *Clipper Jupiter Rex*) belonged to Pan American World Airways, who referred to the type as a 'Super 7'. The longer engine nacelles and saddle tanks for extra fuel are apparent in this excellent photograph.

Eastern Air Lines was one of a number of US domestic trunk carriers which had their Douglas DC-7Bs delivered without the additional nacelle fuel tanks. This Eastern DC-7B was registered N801D and has Wright R-3500-18DA-4 TC engines, but is not fitted with nacelle saddle tanks.

South African Airways Douglas DC-7B, ZS-DKE, which operated a Johannesburg London service in a time of 21 hours. Total fuel capacity for a DC-7B fitted with saddle tanks as seen here was 6,460 US gallons and the gross weight was 126,000lb.

About to refuel here at London Heathrow in 1966 is a DC-7B of the Danish airline Internord. Registered OY-AND, this machine was powered by R-3350-18DA-4 Turbo-Compounds but did not have nacelle-mounted fuel tanks. The contemporary Shell BP fuel bowset and trailer are noteworthy.

Another DC-7B minus nacelle fuel tanks was SE-ERD of Transair, Sweden. It has the standard four R-3350-18DA-4 radial Turbo-Compounds and four-blade paddle propellers as fitted to DC-7Bs. Its name, marked under the cockpit, is *Norrkoping*.

Men of aviation history and destiny. On the left, Britain's Air Commodore Frank (later Sir Frank) Whittle, the great jet pioneer, and on the right, Donald W Douglas, founder of the Douglas Aircraft Co. No doubt Douglas was by then aware that the days of large piston-engined airliners were numbered as jet engines began providing the power for a new breed of aircraft.

Because its DC-7Bs could not fly non-stop westbound across the Atlantic due to prevailing winds, PanAm requested an update from Douglas that could. This emerged as the DC-7C with a range of 4,605 miles (max payload) powered by four 3,400hp R-3350-18EA-1 Turbo-Compound engines. The extra range was attained by adding fuel tanks in a new section inserted between the fuselage and inner nacelles. This increased the wingspan by 10ft, the engines being moved further outboard which reduced noise and vibration in the passenger cabin. A further 42in 'stretch' was added to the fuselage and the gross weight was now 143,000lb. The DC-7C first flew on 20 December 1955 and the prototype (N70C) is seen here on a test flight from Santa Monica in Douglas company colours. The DC-7C was the world's first truly long-range commercial transport and as such was aptly named the Douglas 'Seven Seas'.

Norwegian-registered DC-7C LN-MOE *Reidar Viking* of the Scandinavian Airlines System (SAS). Powered by four 3,400hp R-3500-18EA-1 Turbo-Compounds, this particular aircraft established a world record for the Los Angeles to Stockholm flight. This feat is recorded beneath the pilot's window.

The four R-3500-18EA-1 Turbo-Compounds on this PanAm DC-7C are pushing it along at a cruising speed of some 355mph. Its registration is N731PA and the aircraft carries the name *Clipper Bald Eagle*. 'Super 7' is proudly emblazoned across the fin and rudder.

The extra fuel saddle tanks atop the R-3350-18EA-1 Turbo-Compound engines are prominent in this view of OO-SFC, a Douglas DC-7C owned by Sabena. This photograph was taken on 19 July 1966 according to the photographer's notes. Sabena's initial S and crest on the fin are supplemented by 'Douglas DC-7c Seven Seas' written below it.

Another high-flyer, this time LN-MOD *Guttorm Viking* of SAS, a DC-7C wearing the airline's blue and white colour scheme. The trio of crests aft of the rear passenger windows indicate that Denmark, Norway and Sweden formed Scandinavia's joint airline.

The first of ten new Douglas DC-7Cs delivered to Britain's BOAC between 1956 and 1957 was G-AOIA, seen here on a pre-delivery flight off the Californian coast. Written under the cockpit is the name 'Seven Seas'. The engines are four R-3350-18EA-1 Turbo-Compounds with four-blade propellers.

Ten Douglas DC-7Cs, purchased second-hand from Sabena and PanAm by Caledonian Airways and Trans Meridian, were flown from 1961. This was Caledonian's G-ARYE *Flagship Bonnie Scotland* in 1963, an ex-Sabena machine (OO-SFG) which was sold to Germany in March 1966 as D-ABAR.

Pictured at London, Heathrow, during 1959 this Douglas DC-7C (HB-IBM) is in the unmistakable red and white colour scheme of Switzerland's national airline, Swissair. Across its lower fin and rudder is the name 'Seven Seas'.

Outside its parent company's hangar at London Heathrow in 1958, this Douglas DC-7C of PanAm, N755PA *Clipper East Indian*, is having its upper wing surfaces hosed down by maintenance staff. On its upper vertical tail surfaces is the US flag, the Douglas emblem and the name 'Super 7'.

A busy scene at London Heathrow in the 1960s as I-DUVB, a Douglas DC-7C of the Italian airline Alitalia, takes on fuel from a bowser and trailer while other servicing is carried out inside the aircraft. This particular photograph shows clearly the refuelling points of the DC-7's wing tanks.

As airlines began to equip with pure jet fleets from 1958 onwards, DC-7 series machines were often converted for freighting. Typical was this DC-7B/F (N394AA) in service with American Airlines AIR freight in the 1960s. As can be seen, this aircraft has no saddle fuel tanks.

Three DC-7Cs were converted by UTA as DC-7AMOR observation aircraft on French space programmes, studying satellite-launching, tracking and re-entry. As seen on this DC-7AMOR, radomes were fitted above and below the fuselage, together with interior electronics and radar equipment. The aircraft had a crew of eleven.

Approaching London Heathrow on finals between 1960 and 1964 is a BOAC DC-7CF freighter, G-AOIJ. It went initially to BOAC as a DC-7C in April 1957, but was converted for cargo duties in 1960. Eventually this aircraft returned to the USA in 1965 to become N16465.

Acknowledgements

The author wishes to express his gratitude for the tremendous assistance rendered by the following individuals and concerns in the preparation of this book.

For the use of photographs from their lists, Brian Pickering of Military Aircraft Photographs (MAP) and Brian Stainer of Aviation Photo News (APN). Also Roger Wasley for the use of some of his photographs.

I am especially indebted to Harry Gann of McDonnell Douglas for his great help in providing both photographs and information.

The following airlines' PRO staff proved very generous in providing detailed literature and/or photograph prints: Aer Lingus, Air France, Ansett-ANA, British Airways, Delta Airlines, Eastern Airlines, KLM Royal Dutch Airlines, Northwest Orient, Pan American World Airways, Qantas, Sabena Belgian World Airways, Scandinavian Airlines System and Trans World Airlines.

As always, I am grateful for the patience of my wife, Jean, while I was 'away' in the study and to our cat for keeping me company there.